IAN TAYLOR

FAMOUS DISCOVERIES AND THEIR DISCOVERERS

Fascinating facts from the worlds of science, technology and human achievement

IAN TAYLOR

FAMOUS DISCOVERIES AND THEIR DISCOVERERS

Fascinating facts from the worlds of science, technology and human achievement

MEREO

Cirencester

Mereo Books

1A The Wool Market Dyer Street Cirencester Gloucestershire GL7 2PR
An imprint of Memoirs Publishing www.mereobooks.com

Famous Discoveries and their Discoverers: 978-1-86151-301-4

First published in Great Britain in 2015
by Mereo Books, an imprint of Memoirs Publishing

Copyright ©2015

The address for Memoirs Publishing Group Limited can be found at
www.memoirspublishing.com

The Memoirs Publishing Group Ltd Reg. No. 7834348

The Memoirs Publishing Group supports both The Forest Stewardship Council® (FSC®) and
the PEFC® leading international forest-certification organisations. Our books carrying both the
FSC label and the PEFC® and are printed on FSC®-certified paper. FSC® is the only
forest-certification scheme supported by the leading environmental organisations including
Greenpeace. Our paper procurement policy can be found at
www.memoirspublishing.com/environment

Typeset in 10.5/16pt Bembo
by Wiltshire Associates Publisher Services Ltd. Printed and bound in Great Britain by
Printondemand-Worldwide, Peterborough PE2 6XD

PREFACE

This book deals with a variety of interesting discoveries, mainly relating to the sciences, medicine and geography. There are a few surprises (for example, that Christopher Columbus was not the discoverer of the American continent). I hope this information will be of use to students and that the book will be stocked by libraries. Details regarding the lives of the most famous discoverers, such as Einstein, Newton and Fleming, may interest many readers.

Ian Taylor | February 2015

CONTENTS

Absolute Zero (1862)
Baron Kelvin of Largs
(Sir William Thomson) (1824-1907)

Lord Kelvin was the first to point out that there is an absolute minimum temperature. His ideas followed the acceptance of Charles' Law. In 1787 Charles said that if a gas is cooled, each degree of cooling leads to the volume decreasing by 1/273 of the volume at 0°C. Hence it was argued that a gas at -273°C should have a volume of zero. Early in the 1860s, William Thomson - who had recently been elevated to the peerage as Lord Kelvin - decided it was the average molecular energy of a gas that decreased by 1/273 for each degree of cooling. This means that at -273°C the energy (not the volume) of a gas is 0. Thus -273°C is the lowest temperature possible, known as absolute zero. (In 1905 the German Hermann Nernst showed that it is not a substance's energy that becomes zero at absolute zero, but a related property, entropy.)

William Thomson was horn in Belfast, where his father was a professor of engineering. He matriculated at Belfast at the age of ten, and studied at Cambridge University from 1841 to 1845. In 1845 he went to Paris, to work for a time in Regnault's laboratory. After this - and for the rest of his life - he was Professor of Natural Philosophy at Glasgow. His interest in philosophy had been kindled by the enthusiasm for it at the University of Belfast.

Lord Kelvin showed an interest in theory and in instrumentation. His principal concerns were applying the concepts of mechanics to physics and developing sensitive measuring devices. A galvanometer (current measurer) which he designed led, in 1865, to the efficient working of a submarine telegraph cable between Ireland and Newfoundland. He was knighted for this achievement. ln his later years, he was rather conservative in outlook; for example, he suggested X-rays were probably a hoax and that radio had no future.

He died in 1907 at Largs, a resort on the Firth of Clyde, Scotland. At that time he was generally regarded as the founder of modern physics.

See: Charles' Law, Entropy.

Acetylcholine (1914)

Sir Henry Dale (1875-1968)

Henry Dale, an English physiologist, was the first to extract this compound. He obtained it from ergot, the fungus *Claviceps purpurea*, a parasite of rye and other cereals. ln 1914 he described some of the effects of acetylcholine on living organisms. Many resembled the effects of stimulating the vagus nerve (the tenth cranial nerve and the most important part of the sympathetic nervous system). In 1921 a German researcher, Otto Loewi, found acetylcholine in frogs' hearts. Experiments made it clear that acetylcholine is involved in the transmission of nerve impulses. It is released at nerve endings in voluntary muscle tissue and throughout the autonomic nervous system.

Dale and Loewi shared the Nobel Prize for Physiology in 1936 in recognition of their separate, hut related, significant contributions to understanding the chemical transmission of nerve impulses.

Adenosine Triphosphate (ATP) and Respiration (1937)

Fritz Albert Lipmann (1899-1986)

Lipmann was a German–American biochemist who researched intensively into cell metabolism. In 1937 he was working in Denmark, at the Carlsberg Foundation, Copenhagen, where he accidentally made a discovery of great significance. This was that phosphates are necessary for cells to get energy. It soon became clear that all living cells contain the compound ADP, adenosine diphosphate. This is easily converted to ATP, like this:

$$ADP + phosphate + energy > ATP$$

ATP acts as a reserve of energy. The change shown above can reverse very rapidly, releasing energy. The ATP is broken down to ADP, which subsequently builds up again to ATP. Lipmann was awarded the Nobel Prize for Physiology in 1953. It is strange that this award was not for his work on ADP and ATP, but for research into enzyme chemistry.

See: Krebs Cycle

Adrenaline (1901)

Jokichi Takamine (1854-1922)

Takamine was the first to isolate a pure hormone. The substance is known as adrenaline in Britain. In the USA the correct name is epinephrine, but the trade name adrenalin is often used. In 1894 Schäfer and Oliver, in London, showed that an extract of adrenal gland would make a dog's blood pressure rise. It was not until 1901 that the chemical responsible was isolated, by Takamine. Born in Takaoka, Japan, he graduated in 1879 in Tokyo as a chemical engineer. In 1887 he was responsible for the building of Japan's first superphosphate works and in 1890 he moved to the USA, establishing a laboratory at Clifton, New Jersey.

Adrenaline has become famous as the 'fight or flight' hormone. Its ability to give people above normal strength was dramatically demonstrated at Tampa, Florida, in 1960. Mrs Maxwell Rogers, weighing 55.8 kg (8st 11lb), was near her teenage son when he was working underneath the family car. Suddenly the jack collapsed, trapping her son under the 1.6 tonne (3600 lb) vehicle. Mrs Rogers rescued him by raising one end of the car. The effort cracked some of her vertebrae.

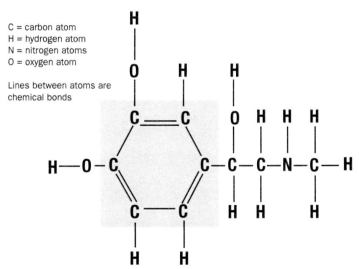

C = carbon atom
H = hydrogen atom
N = nitrogen atoms
O = oxygen atom

Lines between atoms are chemical bonds

Structure closely resembles that of tyrosine, from which it is derived in the body.
Tyrosine is an amino-acid (See: Amino-Acids)
Shaded arae is a benzene ring. (See: Benzene Ring)

AIDS (Acquired Immune Deficiency Syndrome) (1981)

Michael Gottlieb (1947-) and Wayne Shandera (1942-)

Gottlieb was a doctor at the University of California at Los Angeles, while Shandera was a physician with the Los Angeles County Department of Public Health. In 1981 they were surprised to encounter five cases of a very rare form of pneumonia (caused by the organism *Pneumocystis curinii*). The patients were young, gay men, living in the same area, and all became ill at the same time. On 5th June 1981, the journal *Morbidity and Mortality Weekly Report* included an article from the doctors entitled 'Pneumocystic Pneumonia – Los Angeles'. On 4th July 1981 the same journal reported the findings concerning patients with Kaposi's sarcoma, a rare type of skin cancer. The syndrome usually affects men in their seventies, but all the patients were young. They were also gay. Twenty were from New York City and six were from California. Four of the men also had pneumocystic pneumonia, of which ten new cases had been reported in California since the publishing of the June article.

The experts were baffled, and an investigation task force was quickly set up by the Centers for Disease Control (CDC) at Atlanta, Georgia. In August 1981 a link between pneumocystic pneumonia and Kaposi's sarcoma was confirmed. In 1982 the CDC identified AIDS.

Gottlieb and Shandera could have had no idea of the sinister significance behind their report of June 1981. Between 1981 and 1984 over six thousand cases of AIDS were reported. By 1987, according to the World Health Organisation, between five and ten million people had been infected with the virus.

See: HIV.

Air is a Mixture (1775) and Significance of Oxygen (1776)

Antoine Laurent Lavoisier (1743-1794)

Sometimes described as the Newton of chemistry, Lavoisier also had a great interest in geology, scientific agriculture, finance and social reform. A Parisian throughout his life, he was born into a wealthy family. His mother spoiled him, and after her early death he was pampered by an aunt. In 1763 he obtained a degree in law, but his interest in science had already awakened. The next year he began his first important scientific work - investigating the composition of gypsum, a naturally occurring form of calcium sulphate. From then on he worked prodigiously hard, although troubled for years with chronic indigestion. At the age of twenty-five he was elected to the French Academy of Sciences.

In the same year, 1768, he invested in 'Ferme Générale', a private tax-collecting company. He did not collect any taxes himself but he started working for the company as an administrator. In 1771 - when he was twenty-eight – he married Marie-Anne, the daughter of an executive of the company. At the time his bride had not yet reached her fourteenth birthday, but she became a very supportive and helpful wife. The marriage did not produce any children.

In 1772 Lavoisier commenced experiments which involved heating various substances in air. One substance was diamond, which was found to give off carbon dioxide gas when burned (and nothing else). A diamond for the experiment was given by a Parisian Jeweller, who curiously was said to be absolutely certain that the combustion of a diamond produces carbon dioxide. (Diamond and graphite were found to be different forms of the same element, carbon; this was confirmed by later experiments of others, such as Guyton de

Morveau, who were able to show that diamond could be converted to graphite without a chemical reaction.)

From his first experiments in the early 1770s, Lavoisier came to realise that air is a mixture. Until the seventeenth century, people thought it was a single substance. Then a Flemish scientist, Jan Baptista van Helmont, gained the idea that a number of different gases exist. In 1756, Joseph Black, a Scots chemist, showed that carbon dioxide is a gas differing from air, though a small amount of it is present in air. Ten years later, the Londoner Henry Cavendish discovered hydrogen gas.

Lavoisier's most important experiments were with mercury (quicksilver). He found that when mercury was strongly heated in an enclosed vessel, it combined only with part of the atmosphere. The product, a red powder, floated on the surface of the mercury. The other four-fifths of the atmosphere did not alter or affect the mercury in any way. When Lavoisier carefully scraped off all the red powder and heated it strongly, a colourless gas was given off. He found that combustible substances would burn very brightly in this gas, and a small creature, such as a mouse, became very active if put into a jar of the gas. The active part of the air, the part found to support burning and life, he called 'oxygen'.

Lavoisier saw that his results were perfectly explained by the idea that strongly heated mercury combines with oxygen from the air:

Mercury + Oxygen (from air) > Mercury Oxide

If the product of the combustion is itself strongly heated, it breaks down into mercury and oxygen:

Mercury Oxide > Mercury + Oxygen

Oxygen gas had been discovered in 1771 by Scheele in Sweden and in 1774 by Priestley in England. Priestley visited Lavoisier in Paris during 1774, when Lavoisier saw that he himself had shown definitely that oxygen is present in air. Unfortunately he later displayed a common tendency of his, which was to try to take all the credit for himself. He seems to have attempted to give the idea that he was the discoverer of oxygen, as well as the first person to explain clearly the nature of combustion.

Lavoisier called the inactive four fifths of air 'azote' ('no life') but this gas soon became generally known as nitrogen. It had been discovered in 1772 by a Scottish doctor, Daniel Rutherford.

The behaviour of small mammals in air, in oxygen and in nitrogen was investigated by Lavoisier. It became clear that breathing - like burning - uses up oxygen, which comprises one-fifth of the air.

In 1787 Lavoisier published a memorable book, *Methods of Chemical Nomenclature*. This started the scheme, still used today, of a chemical name giving an indication of the composition of a substance. Two years later he produced *Elementary Treatise on Chemistry*, the first modern textbook on the subject.

In 1793 there arose a general outcry against tax-farmers, who included Lavoisier. Anger against Lavoisier was purposely fuelled by Jean-Paul Marat, a journalist. In 1780, although possessing little understanding of science, he had tried to become a member of the Academy of Sciences. Lavoisier had blackballed him, and Marat wanted revenge. In 1794 Lavoisier was put on trial. He asked for some time to complete some chemical work. The court refused, and he was guillotined on the same day. According to one report, an official told him, 'The Republic has no need of men of science'. *See: Carbon Dioxide, Oxygen.*

Algebra (c. 1700 BC)

Ahmes

Although algebra was introduced to the world by a 9th century medieval Persian mathematician called Muhammad ibn Musa al-Khwarizmi, it was an Egyptian writer named Ahmes who put forward the first recorded algebraic problem 2500 years earlier. ln a papyrus thought to date from around 1700 BC, he wrote: 'a heap, together with one-seventh of itself, totals 19; how big is the heap?' Ahmes solved this without using symbols, which did not come into use until much later. (Today most people would quickly solve the problem by a method such as 'Let size of heap be x, then $x + \frac{1}{7}x$ $1 = 19$, whence $x = 16 \frac{5}{8}$.)

The first person known to have represented numbers by letters - as in modern algebra - was a Dominican monk, Jordanus Nemorarius. This was in Germany, around the year 1220. In the sixteenth century, the French mathematician Francois Viète used consonants to represent known numbers and vowels to represent unknown ones. During the next century, another Frenchman, René Descartes (1596-1650), expanded the solving of problems using equations. He also introduced the convention of using x to represent a single unknown quantity or number.

Descartes is also remembered for revolutionising geometry by showing how it could be dealt with in terms of numbers. In 1854 the English thinker George Boole put logical reasoning into algebraic terms.

See: Boolean Algebra.

Alkali Metals and Alkaline-Earth Metals (1807, 1808)

Sir Humphry Davy (1778-1829)

Davy was born in Penzance, Cornwall, into a very poor household. A lively boy, he did not enjoy the regime and discipline of school, and was glad to leave. He was apprenticed to an apothecary, and as a young man had many interests. One of these was experimenting with gases and their effects. He discovered some of the strange effects of nitrous oxide, still commonly known as 'laughing gas'. It is reported that he realised the anaesthetic property of laughing gas, but did not research into this with an aim of relieving suffering.

In 1798 he was appointed superintendent of the Thomas Beddoes Pneumatic Institution at Clifton, Bristol. This institution investigated gases and their effects. Some of the work of Davy and his co-workers established that inhaling laughing gas gives insensitivity to pain. Most of Davy's working life was spent at the Royal Institution, London. Five years after reading his first textbook on chemistry he became Professor of Chemistry at the Institution. He had gained fame as a brilliant lecturer, and achieved still further fame with his discovery of several metallic elements.

This achievement began in 1807 with lime (calcium oxide), which Lavoisier had thought was an element. Davy passed electricity through heated lime and decomposed it into oxygen gas and a new element, calcium. In the same way, he broke down magnesia into oxygen and magnesium. As lime (CaO) and magnesia dissolve a little in water, giving solutions with alkaline properties, they had been known as 'alkaline-earths'. Hence calcium and magnesium were termed 'alkaline-earth metals'.

Subsequently, Davy discovered two more alkaline-earth metals - strontium, (element number 38) and barium (element number 56). In 1807 he discovered sodium and potassium, two of the 'alkali metals', (metals reacting vigorously with cold water to form hydrogen gas and an alkaline solution). On passing a current through damp, melted potash (KOH), Davy obtained, at one plate, small metallic globules. These were pieces of metallic potassium which exploded when put into water. He is said to have danced around the apparatus in delight. Similar treatment of sodium hydroxide (NaOH) yielded globules of sodium, which he found reacted less violently with water.

In 1815 Davy invented the miners' safety lamp, in which the naked flame would not set tire to firedamp, an explosive mixture of methane gas and air frequently formed in coal mines, He was knighted for this achievement.

Davy married in 1812, but the marriage produced no children and was not a happy one. In 1826 he suffered a stroke, and never fully recovered. Three years later he died in Geneva.

See: Anaesthesia.

α (Alpha) and β (Beta) Rays (1898)
Baron Rutherford of Nelson (Sir Ernest Rutherford) (1871-1937)

In 1896 radioactivity was discovered by Becquerel. He found uranium continuously emitted radiation, some of which was identified as cathode rays. Pierre and Marie Curie in Paris and Rutherford in Cambridge, found streams of rays much less penetrating than the electron streams. Rutherford named the less penetrating radiation α-rays and the electron streams β-rays. In 1900 the Frenchman Villard discovered a third form of radiation, γ- (gamma) rays.

Rutherford's grandfather, a Scotsman, emigrated to New Zealand in 1842. Born near Nelson on South Island, Rutherford was the second of twelve children. In 1895 he was placed second for a scholarship to Cambridge. The winning candidate was keen to marry and settle in New Zealand. The scholarship was offered to Rutherford, who heard the good news while working on his father's farm and declared, "That's the last potato I'll dig". In England he progressed rapidly, and researched with much enthusiasm into radioactivity. He made enormous progress. Around 1907, experiments on firing alpha particles at thin foils of metals convinced him that an atom had a dense central core or nucleus, surrounded by a 'froth' of tiny electrons. This discovery earned him the Nobel Prize for Chemistry in 1908. There was irony in the award, as he saw himself as a physicist, and superior to chemists!

In 1909 he isolated α-particles and found that an -particle is the nucleus of an atom of helium, the second element. This work was begun at McGill University in Montreal, Canada, where he researched for a short period. He returned to New Zealand, married, then came back to England, to work at Manchester University.

The first atomic transmutation was achieved by Rutherford in 1919, when he converted nitrogen into oxygen by bombarding nitrogen with -particles. He was made Professor of Physics at Cambridge University in 1919, and was President of the Royal Society from 1925 to 1930. After 1933 he was strongly anti-Nazi. His achievements were many, though in his own scientific thinking he was a conservative, and saw his work as only of theoretical value. He found it difficult to accept Einstein's theories of relativity, and said of the possible development of atomic power, 'That's all moonshine'.

See: Electromagnetic Waves, Electron, Isotopes, Proton, Radioactivity.

Alzheimer's Disease (1898)

Alois Alzheimer (1864-1915)

Dr Alzheimer, born and educated in Germany, worked for some years at the Bergholzi Clinic in Switzerland. This was a prestigious psychiatric institution, where Carl Jung worked at the same time. The doctor was particularly interested in the dementias of old age. His 1898 detailed review of studies of psychogeriatric illnesses described the first case of what is today termed Alzheimer's disease, a disorder of the brain's neurotransmitters. A man had brought in his fifty-one-year-old wife. She was senile, impaired in several ways, and extraordinarily jealous of her husband. Within a few months the woman had died. Alzheimer found in her brain many tangles of fibres and clusters of degenerated nerve endings.

In 1966 US investigators noted that they were finding the same damage in the brains of some senile middle-aged people. Because of this, this form of pre-senile dementia became known as Alzheimer's disease. In 1991 researchers at St Mary's Hospital, London, discovered a gene giving rise to an inherited form of the illness.

America from Iceland (c. 1000)

Leif Eriksson

Leif Eriksson was the son of Erik the Red. Commanded by the King of Norway to take Christianity to Greenland, he sailed with thirty-six men in a Viking galley. Their first landfall may have been on Labrador or Newfoundland. The second landing was in a place where vines bearing grapes were growing, so Eriksson called the area Vinland. It is thought by some to have been the coastal area between Cape Cod and Nova Scotia. Certainly America had been reached. *See: Greenland from Iceland.*

America from Spain (1492)

Christopher Columbus (1451-1506)

The discoverer of America was born Cristoforo Columbo in Genoa, Italy. A weaver's son, he became a visionary who was certain the east could be reached by sailing to the west. After the fall of Constantinople (Istanbul) in 1453, the west became cut off from Asia and its gold and other treasures. Columbus determined that he would find a short sea route to Asia and bring back both riches and glory to Spain. To the end he maintained he had achieved his goal rather than discovering a new continent. On his second Atlantic voyage, for example, all crew members had to swear they were seeing an Asian coastline. In reality the ships were off the coast of Cuba. Sailors found breaking their oaths were fined, lashed severely or had their tongues cut out.

Sailing across the Atlantic under Columbus was probably a terrifying experience, both as a voyage into the unknown and because of the very harsh conditions. Worse still was his treatment of the 'Indians', which was so cruel that in 1500, after his third Atlantic crossing, he was put under arrest and sent back to Spain in chains.

In the early 1470s Columbus lived quietly, assisting his father in the family weaving business. In 1476 he went to Lisbon, where his eyes were opened to what the world could offer. He married in 1479, and produced two sons, Diego in 1480 and Fernando in 1488. In 1484 he asked the King of Portugal to support a crossing of the Atlantic. The King's response was lukewarm to say the least, and the following year support was asked of Ferdinand and Isabella, the King and Queen of Spain. It was 1492 before backing was given 'to discover islands and mainland in the Ocean Sea'.

A flotilla of three small ships left Palos in August, and in October it reached the Bahamas. Columbus decided he had got to the 'Indies' – a name used at that time to cover south-east Asia, India and Indonesia. His mistake is perpetuated to this day in terms such as 'West Indies' and 'Red Indians'. At the end of October, Cuba was discovered, and in December Columbus found Hispaniola, now the separate states of Haiti and the Dominican Republic.

A second Atlantic crossing was made in 1493. Puerto Rico was discovered, and the following year Cuba and Jamaica were explored. For much of 1494 and 1495, Columbus was the Governor of Hispaniola. As a colonial administrator, he proved to be brutal and inefficient.

ln 1498 the third crossing took place, via the Cape Verde Islands. In July the island of Trinidad was sighted, and in early August the ships explored the mainland American coast along the Parra Peninsula, on the northern coast of Venezuela. On the 15th August 1498, Columbus noted he had discovered 'a very great continent'. In October 1500 he was returned to Spain in chains as a result of his extreme brutality in Hispaniola. However, in December of that year he was well received by the King and Queen.

In 1502 he made his fourth and last crossing, which led to

discoveries along the Central American isthmus. In 1503 he was marooned on Jamaica, to be rescued in 1504, and he arrived at Sanlucar, Spain, in November of that year. He endured very poor health during 1505 and passed away the following year at Valladolid, Spain.

Several places have been named alter the explorer: for example, the town at the northern end of the Panama Canal is 'Colon', meaning Columbus, and its port is 'Cristobal', meaning Christopher. However, the honour of being the first European to see America belongs to Leif Eriksson.

See: America from Iceland, Earth's Circumference and Diameter.

American Coast from England (1578-1579)
Sir Francis Drake (c. 1540-1596)

Sir Francis Drake was the eldest of a family of twelve, born to a Tavistock farmer who became a lay preacher. When he was thirteen he went to sea. At twenty-three he joined a Plymouth-based fleet and sailed on slave ships between West Africa and the West Indies. An attack by Spanish ships on his second voyage to the West Indies led to profound hatred of Spain. In 1572 he became a 'legalised pirate', commissioned by Queen Elizabeth I to raid Spanish vessels. In 1577 he set off to explore South America, capture bounty and circumnavigate the world. As the ships entered the Pacific, Drake's ship, the Golden Hind, became separated from the other vessels. These, believing the Golden Hind had sunk, sailed home.

Drake sailed up the coast of Chile, plundered many Spanish ships and raided the ports of Valparaiso and Callao. He visited what is now San Francisco (claiming the region for the Queen), the

Philippines, the Moluccas and Java. In 1580 he was back in England. Only fifty-six of the original one hundred men on his vessel completed the journey. In 1588 his attacks on Spain and its influence climaxed in the defeat of the Spanish Armada off Plymouth.

There is some doubt in the truth of the story that he continued playing bowls on Plymouth Hoe after the Armada had been sighted. Supposedly he said, 'We have time enough to finish the game and beat the Spaniards afterwards'. He died of a fever on a final expedition to the West Indies and was buried at sea in the Panama area.

Amino Acids (1820)
Henri Braconnot (1780-1855)

In 1820 the Frenchman Henri Braconnot was experimenting by heating various materials with sulphuric acid. One substance he tried was gelatine, obtained from animal connective tissue. The product was a sweet, crystalline solid, which he called 'sucre de gelatine', but he then realised it could not be a sugar, as ammonia (NH_3) could be obtained from it. The compound was in fact the simplest amino acid, now known as glycine (amino–ethanoic acid).

A few weeks later Braconnot obtained a white crystalline substance by heating muscle tissue with sulphuric acid. This he named 'leucine', from the Greek word for white. Each compound has at its end an amine group, NH_2, and a carboxyl or acid group, COOH, hence the name amino acid. Amino acids link together to form peptides, which themselves join up to form proteins.

Braconnot, the son of a lawyer, went to Strasbourg when he

was twenty-one. There he worked as a hospital pharmacist and studied science. ln 1801 he completed his education in Paris, and later became Director of the Botanic Garden at Nancy. He never married, and lived very simply. His only entertainment was reading and the occasional visit to the theatre.

See: Sequence of Amino Acids in Proteins and of Nucleotides in DNA.

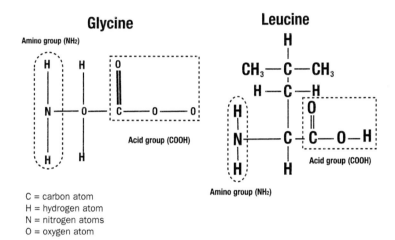

C = carbon atom
H = hydrogen atom
N = nitrogen atoms
O = oxygen atom

Lines between atoms are chemical bonds

Anaesthesia (1844)

Horace Wells (1788-1848)

Drugs to relieve pain have been sought since early times. Alcohol, henbane, mandrake root and opium were tried as general anaesthetics. Sadly, effective doses were found likely to be fatal. ln 1799 Humphry Davy discovered that breathing the gas nitrous oxide made him laugh uncontrollably. This led to 'laughing gas parties' in Britain and USA. These did not lead to any thought of a medical application, only to the name 'laughing gas'. In 1815 Michael Faraday showed ether to be similar in effect to laughing gas, and 'ether parties', similar to laughing gas parties, became fashionable among the young and wealthy.

In 1824 Henry Hickman, a Shropshire doctor, reported success in anaesthetising small mammals with carbon dioxide. The English and French classed him as a crank when he suggested gases could be of use in operations and he died young, totally broken.

It was in America that progress came. In 1842 Crawford Long, a doctor in Georgia, used ether in a minor operation, after attending ether parties. He had noticed that people at the parties who fell over seemed not to be in pain. However, he made no progress with his discovery, which he did not even publicise for seven years. In 1844 a dentist, Horace Wells of Hartford, Connecticut, had a tooth pulled out whilst unconscious with laughing gas. Encouraged, Wells gave public demonstrations using the gas and these were quite successful. In Boston in 1845 during one demonstration, his patient moaned and groaned. He had not received enough gas, but afterwards said he had felt little pain.

Many doctors who had witnessed the operation mocked Wells' efforts. Humiliated, he gave up his work, became a chloroform addict and in 1848 killed himself.

Ether was successfully used in operations by another dentist, William Morton, at the same Boston hospital in which Wells had worked. The first operation using ether took place in October 1846. *See: Chloroform as an Anaesthetic.*

Anaphylaxis (1898)
Charles Robert Richet (1850-1935)

Richet was a professor of physiology in Paris. In 1898 he discovered that dogs reacted as if poisoned when injected with eels' blood serum. In 1902 he obtained similar results by injecting dogs with tiny doses of poison taken from the Portuguese man-of-war jellyfish. He had discovered allergic reaction in the form of 'anaphylactic shock'. The body can form antibodies against a non-harmful protein entering the body and may react violently to any further entry of the protein. Richet won the 1913 Nobel Prize for Medicine for his work. As well as being a physiologist, he was a writer, dramatist and aviation pioneer.

Anatomy (c. 290 BC)
Herophilus of Chalcedon (C. 335-280 BC)

In ancient Greece, animals and occasionally people were dissected. The first true anatomist was a Greek, Herophilus, who started a school of anatomy in Alexandria, Egypt. His star pupil was Erasitratus of Chios, who noted the main parts of the brain and suggested that the heart was a pump. Herophilus was the first to investigate the brain scientifically, recognising it as the seat of intelligence. He distinguished arteries from veins and motor nerves from sensory nerves. The duodenum and prostate gland were discovered and named by Herophilus.

Very little is known about the man himself, not even how or where he died. He was a native of Chalcedon, today a suburb of Istanbul. At least eleven treatises were written by him, but none has been preserved.

Angkor Wat (1859)
Henri Mouhot (1826-1861)

Henri Mouhot was a Frenchman who studied philosophy in Russia before developing a passion for photography. He married an Englishwoman and in 1856 moved to Jersey. In 1858 he sailed for Thailand and met the King of Thailand and the King of Cambodia. In Cambodia, whilst following his interest in animals and fishes, he came across the massive ruins of Angkor Wat, enveloped in jungle growth. The temple system was built by the Kymers, who flourished between the ninth and thirteenth centuries. It is the largest religious building ever constructed, and was abandoned in 1432. Mouhot died of jungle fever in late 1861 whilst journeying to Luong Prabang in Laos.

Antimatter (1930)
Paul Adrien Maurice Dirac (1902-1984)

Dirac was an English theoretical physicist who argued that every atomic particle should have an 'antiparticle'. Thus an 'antiproton' is identical to a proton, but has the opposite charge (negative); an 'antineutron' is identical to a neutron, but has reversed spin direction. In 1932 the existence of 'antielectrons' (positrons) was demonstrated, and in 1955 the existence of 'antiprotons'.

Antimatter was not created in the laboratory until December 1996, when nine atoms of antihydrogen were made at Geneva, Switzerland. Antimatter may exist in parts of the universe. If matter meets antimatter, both are at once annihilated, with a massive release of energy. In *Star Trek*, the US science fiction TV series, spaceships get energy in this way. One day this could happen.

Dirac read electrical engineering at Bristol University, but changed to study mathematics when he was nineteen. In 1926 he was awarded a PhD at Cambridge, and by 1932 he was Lucasian Professor of Mathematics at Cambridge (a post that Isaac Newton had held). He was married to the sister of Eugene Wigner, a noted Hungarian–American physicist.

See: Electron, Neutron, Positron, Proton.

Antitoxins (1890)

Emil Adolf von Behring (1854-1917)

Emil von Behring was a German army doctor who thought microbes could cause the body to make a defensive substance or 'antitoxin'. In 1890 he infected animals with diphtheria, leading to antitoxins being formed in their blood serum. The serum was injected into a boy suffering from diphtheria. The child quickly recovered, and immunisation against the disease was adopted almost at once. In 1892 he discovered immunisation against tetanus (lockjaw). He qualified in 1880, became an army surgeon and in 1889 went to work with Koch in Berlin. For a time he worked with Ehrlich, but they parted in anger. He was honoured in 1894 by a chair at the University of Halle, and in 1901 by the award of the first Nobel Prize for Medicine and Physiology.

See: Bacteriological Techniques, Salvarsan.

Artificial Radioactivity (1935)

Irène Joliot-Curie (1897-1956) and
Frédéric Joliot-Curie (1900-1958)

Irène was Marie and Pierre Curie's daughter. ln 1918 she became her mother's assistant at the Paris Radium Institute. Here she married a co-researcher, Frédéric Joliet. Nobel fame came their way after they produced artificial radioactivity by bombarding aluminium with α-particles. This gave rise to protons and positrons, and positrons continued to be emitted after bombardment had stopped.

Irène's solo studies of radioactive isotopes by firing neutrons at uranium became crucial to the work of Meitner and Hahn nuclear fission. Frédéric investigated the chain reaction, a vital feature of nuclear weapons. ln I939 they stopped releasing papers about the work because of its implications, One paper stating how a nuclear reactor could be developed was kept under wraps until 1949. After the Second World War, Frédéric became scientific head of the Atomic Energy Commission. His wife succeeded Marie Curie as Director of the Radium Institute. She concentrated on pacifist causes until dying at the age of fifty-nine from leukaemia.

See: α and β rays, Nuclear Fission, Positron.

Atom (450 BC)

Leucippus of Miletus (f. 450 BC) and Democritus of
Abdera (r. 460-370 BC)

Early Greek thinkers pondered as to whether matter is continuous or made up of tiny parts. Leucippus and his pupil Democritus decided that even with magic eyes and a magic knife, it would not be possible to chop up matter indefinitely into smaller and smaller bits. Eventually, they reasoned, very tiny indivisible particles would be obtained. Democritus put forward the name 'atom' (not divisible). Amazingly, anticipating ideas that would not come until centuries later, he suggested that different materials contain different atoms, and that it should be possible to convert one substance into another by rearranging its atoms.

The atomic concept was rejected by Plato, Aristotle and other philosophers of the time. It survived only in the writings of Epicurus of Samos (f. 341-270 BC), and in the poem 'On the Nature of Things'. This was written in about 60 BC by Lucretius, a Roman. The poem is said to have been one of the first works to be printed in the Middle Ages.

See: Atomic Theory.

Atomic Masses (weights) (1828)
Baron Jöns Jacob Berzelius (1779-1848)

Berzelius, a Swede, systematically deduced the relative weights of atoms. In 1828 he published a table of 'atomic weights', today known as 'relative atomic masses'. It was years before his results were accepted. He also drew up a classification of minerals based on chemical structure. This established the silicates as a group, following his discovery that silica is an acidic oxide. Silicates are the most important group of compounds in the Earth's crust. Berzelius worked out the symbols for atoms used today, and discovered the elements cerium, selenium, silicon and thorium. By 1830 he was the world's greatest authority on chemistry.

His parents died when he was a boy, and his stepfather saw to his education. He went to medical school, where he excelled in physics. At fifty-six he married a woman of twenty-four. The King of Sweden gave him a baronetcy as a wedding present.

Atomic Theory (1804)

John Dalton (1766-1844)

As early as 1816 an English doctor, William Prout, suggested that all atoms are built up from the hydrogen atom. It was a century before the basic sense of his idea was accepted. The single most important physical science theory of the nineteenth century was Dalton's atomic theory, which said that all matter is made up of invisible atoms. Each element has its own type of atom. Atoms can join up with one another, in definite ratios, to form compound atoms - today known as molecules. Thus a molecule of water is H_2O - two hydrogen atoms linked up with one oxygen atom.

Dalton was the son of a Quaker weaver. In 1793 he moved from Kendal to Manchester, where he worked as a teacher. As well as chemistry, he was keenly interested in meteorology, butterflies and plants. He suffered from red-green colour-blindness, which for many years was known as Daltonism. In habits, he was very regular. For example, every Thursday afternoon he played bowls, and every day he carried out a series of meteorological observations.

See: Atom, Electron, Proton.

Australia from Netherlands (1616)

Dirck Hartog

Hartog, a Dutch mariner, was one of the first to challenge Portuguese supremacy in the East Indian trade. In 1616 his vessel, *Eendracht*, took a new route around Africa, and was swept off course. She landed on an island, 'Dick Hartog's Island' off Shark Bay, on the west coast of Australia. This was the first of several, mainly accidental, landings in the area by the Dutch. The most important sighting was by François Thyssen in 1627. He was the first to sail into the Great Australian Bight. The first Dutch settlers came in 1629 to what is today Northampton, north of Perth, The area was called New Holland, but was not thought to be of any particular value.

Australopithecus africanus (1924)

Raymond Arthur Dart (1893-1988)

ln 1924 blasting at a limestone quarry near Taungs, South Africa, led to a small skull being exposed. The workers thought it was human-like and the manager sent it to Dart in Johannesburg, who at once identified it as an intermediate between ape and man and gave it its name, which means 'southern ape of Africa'. When the news got out, anthropologists felt he was mistaken. However, Robert Broom, a Scottish expert living in South Africa, was sure human beings had originated in Africa. He quickly confirmed Australopithecus as the nearest thing to a missing link yet found. It lived over two million years ago, made stone tools and killed animals for food.

Dart was born and educated in Australia and graduated as a doctor in 1917. In 1923 he moved to South Africa, and became a well-known surgeon and anatomist, holding a chair at Witwatersrand University.

See: Homo erectus.

Australopithecus boisei (1959)

Mary Leakey (1913-1996)

For many years in the mid 20th century, a Kenya-born Englishman, Louis Leakey, and Mary, his English wife, combed promising areas of Eastern Africa for early fossil hominids. In 1959, their twenty-six years of searching were rewarded by a discovery by Mary in the Olduvai Gorge, Tanzania. She came across skull fragments which were found to come from an upright walking hominid which was closer to man than to the apes. The find, known as *Australopithecus boisei* (after C. Boise, who funded research), was not thought by Louis Leakey to be in the direct line of ancestry to modern humans.

Mary and Louis Leakey were involved in the discoveries of several early hominids, such as *Homo habilis* ('handy man') in 1960. After Louis died in 1972, Mary continued to search. A few years later her team found the footprint trail of a hominid dating back over three million years.

See: Australopithecus africanus.

Aztec Empire from Spain (1520)

Hernán Ferdinand Cortés (1485-1547)

Hernán Cortés was the most famous Spanish conquistador, and the conqueror of Mexico. When he was nineteen he sailed in 1504 to Hispaniola. In 1511 he joined an expedition of three hundred which sailed to conquer Cuba. Appointed King's Treasurer in Santiago da Cuba, he was soon in danger of losing his position due to womanising. In 1519 he was leader of a colonising expedition to look into indications of Aztec wealth. These had come from a 1518 voyage from Santiago by another Spaniard, Juan de Grijalva. The expedition reached Yucatan, where a fight took place at Tabasco. The Yucatanis had not seen horses before, and took soldiers on horseback to be centaurs.

Cortés realised great wealth must be at the heart of the Aztec Empire, and set of for Montezuma, its king, and the city of Tenochtitlan, now Mexico City. Before leaving, he ensured commitment to the venture by burning his boats on the Mexican beaches. Cortés and his men were greatly impressed by the vast amounts of gold, silver and treasure in the city, and by the temple of Huitzilopochtli. This had been dedicated in 1486 by sacrificing seventy thousand victims. Human sacrifice by priests was an integral part of Aztec culture. Montezuma was seized as a hostage to subdue the Aztecs. The king had greeted Cortés with uncharacteristic politeness. It appeared that the white 'god-man' Quetzalcoatl – long forecast in Aztec legends – had at last come. Relations between Aztecs and Spaniards rapidly worsened, and suddenly Cortés had to hurry to the coast to quell a revolt. He returned to find violent conflict in progress. Montezuma was stoned to death by his own people whilst he pleaded for the conquerors to be placated. The Spanish withdrew, but in 1521 Cortés returned to vanquish Tenochtitlan, and with it the Aztec civilisation.

Cortés led an expedition into California in 1536, returned for good to Spain in 1540 and died, poor and disillusioned, seven years later. *See: Peru from Spain.*

Bacteriological Techniques (1875-1906)
Robert Koch (1843-1910)

Koch was one of a family of thirteen. In 1866 he graduated in medicine from Göttingen. He worked as an army surgeon, then became a Prussian country doctor. He discovered how to find which types of bacteria cause which diseases, as well as ways of identifying bacteria and of growing them in pure cultures (without contamination).

He discovered the bacteria causing anthrax, cholera and tuberculosis. By the end of the century most disease–causing bacteria had been identified by Koch or one of his many students. He also showed that bubonic plague is transmitted by a louse which infests rats, and sleeping sickness by the tsetse fly. During his very active life, Koch married twice. In 1885 he became a professor in Berlin, and in 1905 he was awarded a Nobel Prize.

See: Germ Theory of Disease.

Bacteriophages (1915)
Frederick William Twort (1877-1950)

Bacteriophages ('bacteria eaters') are a group of viruses which attack and destroy bacteria, especially in the intestine. They were discovered in 1915 by Twort, an English bacteriologist. A Canadian,

Felix d'Hérelle, who independently discovered them in 1915, gave them their name.

Twort, who was born and died at Camberley, Surrey, was Professor of Bacteriology at London University.

Bee Language (1960)
Karl von Frisch (1886-1982)

Von Frisch, an Austrian naturalist and zoologist, is noted for his studies of honey bees. He found that their 'dances' on the honeycombs informed other bees of the directions, distances and amounts of food sources. They could tell directions from the polarisation of light in the sky. Some colours, including ultraviolet, could be distinguished by bees.

Von Frisch was born in Vienna, and studied there and then in M nich, where he obtained a doctorate in 1910.

Benzene Ring (1865)
Friedrich August Kekulé von Stradonitz (1829-1896)

Benzene was discovered by Michael Faraday in 1825 whilst investigating problems in bottling gases under pressure, but it was forty years before its chemical structure was discovered. Experiments soon showed that the formula is C_6H_6, ie the benzene molecule has six atoms of carbon and six of hydrogen. No one could explain the structure until Kekulé, half asleep on a bus, saw a chain of carbon atoms forming a coil, like a snake biting its tail. He woke up, possibly muttering 'Eureka!' His concept of a six-membered ring of atoms of carbon proved correct. Substances that contain the benzene ring – 'aromatic compounds' – are very important in biochemistry.

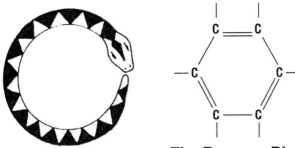

The Benzene Ring

Kekulé von Stradonitz set out to be an architect, but the famous Liebig drew him to the delights of chemistry. After scientific travels in England and France, he returned to Heidelberg, Germany. Here he lectured, set up a private laboratory and took the chair of chemistry. Finally he became a professor at Ghent, Belgium.

See: Tracers.

Beriberi - Prevention and Cure (1891)

Admiral Takaki

Admiral Takaki of the Japanese Navy brought to an end the scourge of beriberi in his ships simply by introducing vegetables to the sailors' monotonous rice diet. No one could explain the result. In 1896, experiments in Jakarta by a Dutch physician, Christiaan Eijkman, confirmed that chickens stayed healthy if fed unhulled rice, but developed polyneuritis, resembling human beriberi, if fed polished rice. Eijkman was unsuccessful in isolating from rice hulls the compound combating beriberi. The compound vitamin B, or thiamine, was first isolated in 1912 in Japan. Its chemical structure was determined in 1934 in the USA.

See: Scurvy - Prevention and Cure, Vitamins.

Big Bang (1927)

Georges Henri Lemaître (1894-1966)

Abbé Lemaître, a Belgian mathematician, proposed in 1927 that the universe had a beginning. He suggested that an enormously dense 'cosmic egg' had exploded in what became known as the 'big bang', and suggested that the galaxies were still rushing outwards in all directions as a result of that colossal explosion. George Gamow, a Russian–American physicist, elaborated the concept, suggesting that the expansion would continue indefinitely. Lemaître's concept followed work by the Russian Alexander Friedmann, indicating in 1922 that it is not sensible to view the universe as static.

Friedmann's view was proved to be correct in 1965, when Arno Penzias and Robert Wilson, two New Jersey physicists, detected microwave 'noise' from outer space which varied in any direction by less than one part in 10,000. Later, B. Dicke and]. Peebles at the University of Princeton concluded that the early universe was white hot, and if the galaxies were rushing away from one another, the Einstein red shift meant present-day radiation would be microwaves. It was precisely these microwaves that Penzias and Wilson had found.

In 1970, a paper by Stephen Hawking and Roger Penrose showed that if the general theory of relativity is correct, and if the universe contains as much matter as we suppose, the universe started at a singularity with infinite mass and zero volume. The explosion of this singularity led to the universe, and was the beginning of time. Current measurements place this event at 13.8 billion years ago. Hawking, a Cambridge professor, has become world famous for his work, achieved in spite of being very severely incapacitated by motor neurone disease (amyotrophic lateral sclerosis) which began in his early twenties.

The latest indications are that not only will the expansion of the universe continue forever, it is actually speeding up, as a result of the presence of 'dark energy', a phenomenon which is not yet understood.

Abbé Lemaître was born in Charleroi, and in 1914 he entered the army from work in civil engineering. His war service interested him in physics. After qualifying as a priest in 1922, he went on to study astrophysics at Cambridge University and the Massachusetts Institute of Technology. Later he became Professor of Astrophysics at Louvain, where he had been an undergraduate and where he died aged seventy-two.

See: Expanding Universe, Relativity Theories, Space-Time Continuum.

Biochemical Genetics (1942)

George Wells Beadle (1903-1989) and Edward Lawrie Tatum (1909-1975)

In 1941 the US geneticists Beadle and Tatum studied common pink bread mould (*Neurospora crassa*). It produces eight spores, each possessing seven single chromosomes. Exposure to X-rays created mutations which led to observable effects in the behaviour of the spores. Further work showed that the formation of an enzyme (biological catalyst) is due to a particular gene, which is a segment of a chromosome. Beadle obtained a PhD at Cornell University on the genetics of maize. He went on to investigate eye colours in the fruit fly. His colleague Tatum helped in deducing how genes operate, and later was involved in increasing the efficiency of penicillin production. The two researchers shared a Nobel Prize in 1958 tor their work on gene function.

See: DNA and RNA.

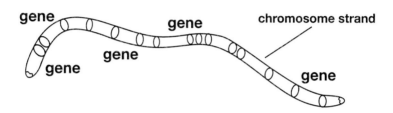

The difference between a gene and a chromosome. A gene is a portion of DNA, and a chromosome contains many genes along its length. Note that a trait can involve a single gene, but often more than one gene is involved, for example for colour of hair or for intelligence.

Black Holes (1783)

John Michell (1724-1793)

A region of space-time where gravity is so intense that nothing at all can escape is known as a 'black hole', a term first used in America in 1969. 'Black' signifies that not even light can escape. Early scientists assumed light travels at infinite speed, until Romer showed this is not so (1676). Michell, a Cambridge don, assumed gravity could affect light. He suggested in 1783 that a star could be so dense that its gravitational field would stop any light escaping. Such a body would be invisible and detectable only by its gravitational field. Shortly afterwards, the Marquis de Laplace, in France, independently came up with the same idea.

In 1965 Roger Penrose at Cambridge showed that a star collapsing under its own gravity is contained in a region whose surface area eventually becomes zero. It becomes a singularity, having maximum mass and a volume of zero; ie, space–time curvature is infinite. At such a point the general theory of relativity breaks down.

Stephen Hawking, Lucasian Professor of Mathematics at Cambridge, studied black holes in the 1970s and showed that it is possible for radiation to be emitted from just outside a black hole.

Michell was a geologist by training. He invented a torsion balance, and suggested how earthquakes start. Sometimes he has been referred to as the father of seismology.

See: Big Bang, Light has a Finite Speed, Pulsars,
Quasars, Relativity Theories.

Blood Groups (1901, 1927 & 1939)

Karl Landsteiner (1868-1943)

In 1900 Karl Landsteiner of Vienna University set out to find out why blood transfusions frequently failed. Using blood samples from himself and five colleagues, he discovered that the blood of some individuals causes the red blood cells of others to clump together. The clumping is due to the presence or absence on red cells of two substances ('antigens') which cause antibodies to be produced. He distinguished blood groups A, B and O, and in 1902 a fourth group, AB. In 1927 he found a further system – the MN blood groups. More important was the Rhesus factor, explained by experiments of Landsteiner and others with transfusions from Indian rhesus monkeys into rabbits and guinea pigs.

From 1926, Landsteiner worked at the Rockefeller Institute for Medical Research in New York. Today blood is routinely checked for its ABO grouping and whether the Rhesus factor is positive or negative. It took a long time for Landsteiner's work to he acknowledged, and it was only in 1930 that he won a Nobel Prize.

Boolean Algebra (1854)
George Boole (1815-1864)

In his 1854 book *An Investigation of the Laws of Thought*, the mathematician George Boole described a system of deductive logic. Logical statements can he represented by symbols, which lead to definite conclusions when manipulated. His work led to 'truth tables', and Boolean algebra has an important role in modern information theory. This in part came from the 1938 discovery by an American, Claude Shannon, that Boolean logic can be handled by binary symbolism and hence by computers.

Boole was born in Lincoln, England, the son of a shoemaker. At sixteen he became a mathematics teacher. In 1835 he set up his own school and fourteen years later he became Professor of Mathematics at the University of Cork, Eire. Pneumonia took his life in Cork at the age of forty-nine.

Brazil from Portugal (1500)

Pedro Alvarez Cabral (c. 1467- c.1520)

Pedro Alvarez Cabral was a Portuguese navigator who commanded his country's second expedition to India. He sailed from Lisbon in 1500 with thirteen ships, taking da Gama's advice to give a wide berth to the becalming seas around the Gulf of Guinea. In fact, Cabral swept out so far that he came to Caravela. He named it 'island of the true cross' but actually he had come to Brazil (named years later after 'pau-brasil', a wood used in dye-making).

Cabral continued to the east, but luck was not with him. Off the Cape of Good Hope, four ships sank, and all on board drowned, including Dias. At Calicut, India, they fought with Muslims and on the way home five more ships foundered.

See: Cape of Good Hope from Portugal, India from Portugal

Brownian Motion (1827)

Robert Brown (1773-1858)

Brown, a Scottish biologist, used a microscope to observe that pollen grains in water dance about erratically. They perform what Einstein called 'drunken man movement'. At first the jiggling was considered to be due to life in the grains, but then it was found that dyestuff particles in water also exhibit the motion. In 1863 particles by surrounding molecules of water. Einstein carried out a theoretical analysis, and showed that it is possible to calculate the size of a molecule of water from the extent of the jiggling. In 1908 the Frenchman Jean Perrin did just this, convincing even the sceptical German chemist Wilhelm Ostwald of the reality of molecules.

In 1831 Brown recognised that a living cell normally has a dense centre, which he named the nucleus ('little nut'). A priest's son, he studied medicine at Cambridge but did not sit for a degree. In 1801 he enjoyed voyaging to Australia as a naturalist. Later in life he became librarian to the Linnaean Society and to Sir Joseph Banks, the botanist on Captain Cook's first major voyage.

Cape of Good Hope from Portugal (1488)
Bartolemeu Dias (c. 1450-1500)

Bartolemeu Dias was a Portuguese navigator who set out in 1487 to find the southern tip of Africa. He got as far as Angra da Roca, now Port Elizabeth, and the Great Fish River (Rio do Infante). On returning, he saw the magnificent cape, which he called the Cape of Storms. This was a sad portent, as he died in a storm off the cape on a second voyage. The King of Portugal renamed the headland the Cape of Good Hope. It was Dias's discovery that led to da Gama making the first voyage from Europe to the East.

See: India from Portugal.

Capillaries (1661)
Marcello Malpighi (1628-1694)

Malpighi, an Italian physician and anatomist, examined the lungs of a frog with a primitive microscope. This was four years after the death of William Harvey. He discovered tiny blood vessels linking arteries with veins, and called them capillaries (from the Latin *capillus* – hair). A professor at Bologna and then Pisa, Malpighi was the first professional anatomist to use a microscope. Named after him are several minute bodily structures, notably the Malpighian bodies of kidney tubules. He produced very accurate descriptions of most tissues and organs of the body.

Malpighi's birthplace was a village near Bologna, and in 1653 he gained a medical degree at Bologna's University. In 1691 he was made private physician to the Pope, and he suffered a fatal illness in Rome three years later.

See: Circulation of Blood.

Carbon-60 (Buckminsterfullerene) (1985)

Sir Harold Kroto (1939-)

Before work done by Kroto of the University of Sussex, and by Robert Curl and Richard Smalley of Houston University, the element carbon seemed to have just two structural forms (allotropes) - diamond and graphite. Wood charcoal, gas carbon and other varieties are often not pure carbon but structurally they all have the graphite type of structure.

In 1985 in Brighton, England, Kroto irradiated some graphite with a laser beam in an atmosphere of the inert gas helium. Condensing gaseous carbon in the inert atmosphere produced C_{60} (a new allotrope with sixty atoms per molecule). It became known as 'buckminsterfullerene', as each molecule resembles a geodesic dome, a shape patented in 1954 by the distinguished American Richard Buckminster Fuller (1895-1983). Molecules of C_{60} look remarkably like soccer balls, and are often called Buckyballs. Recently, further work has led to the finding of further forms – C_{170}, C_{240} and C_{540}, collectively called fullerenes.

Carbon Dioxide (1754)

Joseph Black (1728-1799)

Early in the seventeenth century, the Flemish physician J B van Helmont (1579–1644) realised that fermenting fruit juice gives off a gas that is not air. He was the first to use the term 'gas'. The Scottish chemist Black obtained 'taxed air' (carbon dioxide) by heating carbonates, and discovered its main properties. His 1754 thesis for a medical degree dealt with the reversible formation of the gas and calcium oxide by heating calcium carbonate.

Black, one of a family of thirteen, was born in Bordeaux. His father, a wine merchant, sent him to Britain when he was twelve. He studied medicine at Glasgow and Edinburgh, and later was a professor at each university. In studying heat, Black realised temperature is not the same as quantity of heat, and showed a basic understanding of what we today call specific heat capacity and latent heat. He was one of the pioneers whose studies led to understanding the conservation of energy.

See: Air is a Mixture and Significance of Oxygen,
Conservation of Energy

Cathode Rays (1876) and Channel Rays (1886)

Eugen Goldstein (1850-1930)

When researchers passed electricity through evacuated glass tubes, a green glow was seen on the tube opposite the cathode (negative plate). In 1876 Goldstein, a German physicist, suggested 'cathode rays' emitted from the rays were making the glass glow. He thought they were electromagnetic radiation, but later experiments proved they were beams of electrons, the tiniest negatively charged particles.

In 1886 Goldstein used a cathode ray tube with a perforated cathode, and discovered *Kanalstrahlen* ('channel rays') travelling the opposite way to the cathode rays. Later, Rutherford identified the new rays as streams of positively-charged fundamental particles, the 'opposite numbers' to electrons. In 1914 he gave these the name 'protons'.

Goldstein was born at Gliwice, Poland, (then Gleiwitz, Silesia). He worked at Berlin University, obtaining a doctorate there in 1881. Much of his research was carried out in his private laboratory. He suffered a fatal collapse near his home in Berlin when he was eighty-one.

See: Electron, Proton.

Cell Division (1879)
Walther Flemming (1843-1905)

Flemming, a German anatomist, found he could stain tiny thread-like granules in the nucleus of a living cell with red dyes. The cell was killed, but in a slice of tissue he was able to catch cells at different stages of division. In 1882 he published a book describing the stages of cell division or 'mitosis'; the name came from the Greek for 'thread', given because of the prominent part played by the tiny granules. These in 1888 were termed 'chromosomes ('coloured bodies', although they are colourless in the natural state). Later, each species was shown to have a characteristic number of chromosomes in each cell (twenty-three pairs in human beings). In mitosis, before a cell divides, the number of chromosomes doubles, so each daughter cell has the same number as the parent cell.

In 1885 E. van Bededen, a Belgian embryologist, discovered that the formation of egg and sperm cells involves 'reduction division' or meiosis. Here there is no doubling up before cell division, and egg and sperm cells have half the normal number of chromosomes. A fertilised egg cell has the normal number, half provided by the egg cell and half by the sperm cell. The chromosomes contain the genes, made of DNA.

Flemming graduated in anatomy in 1868, and became a professor at Prague in 1872. In 1876 he took a chair at Kiel, and kept the position for the rest of his working life.

See: *Cell Theory, Sex Chromosomes.*

Cell Theory (1839)

Matthias Jakob Schleiden (1804-1881) and Theodor Schwann (1810-1882)

Biologists gradually came to realise that all living matter is made of cells. In 1824 R. Dutrochet, a French physiologist, pointed out that some life forms are single-celled, whilst most organisms consist of many cooperating cells. However, the theory that the cell is the unit of life became prominent only when stated independently by Schleiden (1838) and by Schwann (1839). Their views appeared at about the same time, Schleiden referring to plants and Schwann to animals.

Schleiden was horn in Hamburg and trained as a lawyer. This did not appeal, and his interest turned to plant life. By 1839 he was Professor of Botany at Jena. Schwann, born in Neuss, Prussia, qualified as a doctor in 1834. Later he held chairs of anatomy in Louvain and Liege, Belgium. In 1834 he discovered the stomach enzyme pepsin, and four years later he showed that fermentation is due to a life process.

Central and East Africa from South Africa (1852-1868)

David Livingstone (1813-1873)

Born in Blantyre, Scotland, Livingstone was one of seven children of a very poor home. His unusual nature surfaced at the age of ten, when he bought a book on Latin grammar with some of his first wage packet. He began work in a cotton mill, but soon became keen to be a missionary in China. In 1840 he was ordained and the next year arrived in Cape Town. A devout and pious Christian, he saw his main task as 'converting the natives'. However, mission stations had to be set up to the north, and soon he was pushing northwards across the Kalahari Desert. In 1843 he founded his own mission at Kolobeng. In 1844 he was attacked and injured by a lion. He married in 1845, and was often accompanied on his early journeys by his wife and three young children. When a fourth child was born on one journey he sent his family back to Scotland, feeling that the hardships of the Kalahari were too much for a family.

Between 1849 and 1856 his travels led to the discovery of Lake Ngami, in the Kalahari, the Cuanza River and the Victoria Falls. Returning to Britain, he was acclaimed as a hero. In 1858 he became the British Consul at Quelimane on the Indian Ocean coast. From there expeditions led to the discovery of Lake Malawi, Lake Mweru and Lake Bangweulu. In 1869 it was unclear what had happened to him. In 1871 he was found by Henry Stanley at Ujiji, who greeted him with the famous statement: 'Dr Livingstone, I presume?' He was in fact very ill and weak, but he accompanied Stanley along the northern part of Lake Tanganyika. When Stanley set off back to the coast, Livingstone went only as far as Tabora. He declined to leave Africa with the Nile's source still not definitely established, and made his way back to Lake Bangweulu. In 1873 he died, close to the source of the Luapula River. His servants had such a regard for him that they buried his heart, to remain for ever in Africa. His body was carried to the coast, a nine-month journey, and in 1874 he was buried in Westminster Abbey, London.

See: Mountains of the Moon from USA.

Chaos Theory (1979)
Mitchell Feigenbaum (1944-)

Feigenbaum, a US mathematician trained as a particle physicist, found a basic similarity in the behaviour of equations relating to a variety of physical and biological systems. His theory became important in describing the underlying scaling constancy in what generally appears as chaotic behaviour. Dr Feigenbaum, who worked mainly in a Los Alamos laboratory, published very little in his earlier days. It was some time before the discovery of this rather eccentric intellectual achieved due prominence, but today the theory is of much scientific interest.

Charles' Law (1787)
Jacques Alexandre César Charles (1746-1823)

A French physicist, Charles is remembered mainly for his meticulous experiments on the volumes of gases when heated or cooled. He found that on warming a gas at constant pressure each degree of heating causes a volume increase of $1/273$ of the volume at $0°C$. On cooling a gas, the volume decreased in the same proportion. It was later suggested that if a gas could be cooled to –

273°C its volume would be zero. This paradox was resolved by Lord Kelvin seventy-five years after the discovery of Charles' Law.

Charles was born at Beaugency, Loiret, and died in Paris, where he had taught at the Sorbonne. In 1783 he made the first hydrogen balloons. He failed to publish his experiments on gases, which were duplicated in 1802 by Gay-Lussac, another Frenchman.
See: Absolute Zero.

Chemical Compositions of Stars

Cecilia Payne-Gaposchkin (1900-1979)

Born in Wendover, Buckinghamshire, Cecilia Payne had a traditional English upbringing, and her parents were dismayed when she decided to become a scientist. At that time women were still considered intellectually inferior to men; at one of the universities where she worked, female staff could not use the main door and had to enter by a side entrance.

After graduating and working initially in Britain, she spent most of her working life in the USA, where she settled with her husband, Sergei Gaposchkin, a Russian-born astrophysicist, raising a son and daughter. Cecilia soon became a respected astrophysicist herself and carried out work which enabled her to relate the spectral classes of stars to their temperatures, showing that the great variation in stellar absorption lines was due to differing amounts of ionization at different temperatures rather than to different elements being present. Her studies showed that hydrogen and helium were the most abundant elements in stars, and therefore in the universe as a whole.

China from Italy (1271-1292)

Marco Polo (1254-1324)

Maffeo and Niccolo Polo, brothers and noblemen from Venice, were the first Europeans to get to Cathay (modern China). Setting out for Constantinople (Istanbul) in 1255, they followed the overland Silk Route. During their 14-year expedition, they met Kublai Khan in Cambaluc (now Beijing). They returned in 1271 and stayed for sixteen years, serving in the court.

It was Niccolo's son, Marco, who became famous as an intrepid adventurer and observer. Marco went with his father and uncle on their second expedition to Cathay. Kublai Khan was very much impressed by the Polos, and retained them as advisers. Marco, who was very quick to master languages, was sent on extensive diplomatic Journeys, travelling as far as Tibet. He also governed the province of Yangchow for three years.

ln 1292 the Venetians were permitted to return home. They went by sea, arriving in Venice three years later. In 1298 Marco Polo was captured in a fight at sea between Venice and Genoa. A writer, Rusticello, was in prison with him, and took down his remembrances. The account aroused great interest. By 1501 there were translations in four languages. The work opened European minds to the existence of an awesome and ancient world.

Several omissions from the accounts are puzzling – no mention is made of the different languages of Cathay, of tea or of the Great Wall of China. *The Travels of Marco Polo* did, however, tell of much of the vastness and splendour of the East. Polo was often accused of wild exaggeration. On his deathbed he protested, 'I have not told one half of what I saw!'

Chloroform as an Anaesthetic (1847)

Sir James Young Simpson (1811-1870)

In 1831 chloroform was discovered almost simultaneously in America, France and Germany. Sixteen years later, Simpson, professor of midwifery at Edinburgh, experimented with it on himself and friends. He had been using ether as an anaesthetic in obstetric cases, but was concerned that it might explode. Soon he had tried out chloroform on about thirty patients. It worked well, but he met with an outcry, mainly from men claiming it was God's will that labour is painful. The use of chloroform was continued however, and the protests ended in 1853 when Queen Victoria took it whilst giving birth to her eighth child, Prince Leopold. The anaesthetist was John Snow, the first full-time British anaesthetist (later to gain fame for demonstrating that cholera is waterborne).

Simpson was born at Bathgate, Linlithgow. He did very well at school, and at fourteen entered Edinburgh University. His final thesis won him an immediate appointment as a professor's assistant. He died in London in 1870, remembered principally for his obstetric use of chloroform.

See: Anaesthesia

Chlorophyll (1817)

Joseph Bienaimé Caventou (1795-1877) and Pierre Joseph Pelletier (1788-1842)

The green colouring matter in plants was isolated in 1817 by the French chemists Caventou and Pelletier. They named it chlorophyll from Greek words meaning 'green leaf'. It was shown to be the catalyst for the vital process of photosynthesis. Chlorophyll has a complicated structure, and it was not until 1960 that it was synthesised in the laboratory. The two chemists went on to discover several specialised plant products, including caffeine, quinine and strychnine.

Caventou and Pelletier made their discoveries at the School of Pharmacy in Paris. Caventou concentrated on research into botanical products and was Professor of Toxicology from 1835 to 1860. Pelletier also held positions as a professor and as assistant financial director of the school.

Circulation of the Blood (1627)

William Harvey (1578-1657)

Englishman William Harvey's publication *On the Motion of The Heart and Blood in Animals* (1628) took time to be generally accepted. Based on many dissections and experiments, it explained the roles of the heart, arteries and veins. Before Harvey there had been much misunderstanding, stemming from Greek ideas. The very name 'artery' came in fact from Greek words meaning 'I carry air' because, in corpses, arteries were found to be empty. Galen, a Greek physician who practised in Rome, did show that arteries carry blood, but his views of the working of the body were full of strange errors.

Harvey was born in Folkestone, Kent, the eldest of a large family. He studied at Cambridge and then at Padua. Here Fabricius, one of his teachers, was the discoverer of valves in veins, but he misconstrued their function. In 1602 Harvey settled in London, and in 1604 he married the daughter of King James I's physician.

Five years later he became physician to St Bartholomew's Hospital. His understanding of the circulation was furthered by meticulous experiments on mammals, snakes and himself. Without a microscope he did not see blood capillaries, which were discovered four years after his death by Malpighi.

Harvey's research extended to embryology, culminating in 1651 with the publishing of *The Generation of Animals*. In later life he became physician to King Charles I, but all was lost when the Royalists were defeated in the English Civil War (1642-1649). He ended up widowed, lodging with one or other of his six brothers and living off his inheritance and his small practice.

See: Capillaries

Circumnavigation of the Earth (1521)
Ferdinand Magellan (b. 1480-1521)

Portuguese-born and bred as Fernão de Magalhães, Magellan became a Spanish citizen in 1517, having fallen out with the King of Portugal. Four years later he set off with five ships to sail round the world. Sailing to South America, he eventually found the strait between the subcontinent and Tierra del Fuego. Thirty-eight days of travel through the 370 mile (595 km) strait led him to an ocean, which he named the Pacific. There were now only three vessels. One ship had been wrecked and another deserted. As they crossed the Pacific, no one caught sight of any of its many islands. After ninety-nine days without fresh water or fresh food they landed at Guam. The ships sailed on to the Philippines and Cebu. On an island called Mectan, near Cebu, a pointless invasion led to a fight with the inhabitants. Magellan and forty of his men were killed.

The one hundred and fifteen survivors get away in two ships, reaching Moluccas in late 1521. One vessel, commanded by Juan Sebastian del Cano, reached Spain in 1522 via the Indian Ocean and the Cape of Good Hope. This ship was the first to sail around the world.

See: Earth's Circumference and Diameter.

Coelacanth (1938)

J.L.B. Smith (1897-1968)

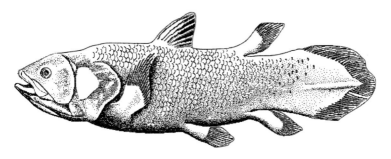

COELACANTH

(Latimeria chalumnae)

Heavy bodied and up to two metres long. Has fleshy limb-like fins and a small extra tail. Lives in waters 100-300m deep.

In December 1938 a South American trawler working off the east coast of South Africa brought up a 1.5m (5ft) long fish which had fins joined to fleshy lobes instead of directly to the body. The body was shown to Dr Smith, a zoologist, who recognised it as a coelacanth, a fish thought to have been extinct for seventy-five million years. It is a primitive fish similar to that from which the first amphibians developed.

Several more coelacanths have since been brought to the surface, and later a separate population of a different species was found in the seas off Indonesia. Coelacanths are deep-water creatures and cannot survive for long at sea level.

Conditioned Reflexes (1903)
Ivan Petrovich Pavlov (1849-1936)

Pavlov, a Russian surgeon and psychologist, created artificial channels in dogs leading from digestive organs to the outside. This was to allow him to observe gastric juice being secreted. Intriguingly, he found secretion occurred at the sight or smell of meat, or even hearing him approaching. Noticing the dogs salivating as he drew near with food, he sounded a bell as it was given. After twenty to forty associations, just ringing the bell would cause salivation. This was an instance of a conditioned reflex. In further experiments, dogs learned to associate food with a circle of light and no food with an ellipse of light. The dogs were very disturbed when the ellipses were made almost circular.

The experiments were attempts to show an absence of free will, which Pavlov did not consider people to have. He thought that mental events were reflex actions. In 1913 John Watson in the USA founded 'behaviourism', which takes reflexes as the basic unit to explain all behaviour and sees even complex human behaviour as a summation of simple conditioned reflexes. The leading exponent of the tenet that conditioning produces our behaviour was another American, B F Skinner.

Conservation of Energy (1847)

Hermann Ludwig Ferdinand von Helmholtz (1821-1894)

In 1841 a British physicist, James Joule, indicated the equivalence of heat and mechanical energy. Six years later von Helmholtz, a German physicist and physiologist, realised we can convert energy from one form (eg sound) to another (eg heat), but we cannot create or destroy it. This is the law of the conservation of energy, which he was the first to enunciate clearly and formulate mathematically.

Many modern devices are concerned with converting energy into a different form (eg the electric motor converts electrical energy into energy of motion or mechanical energy). Today we know matter and energy are interconvertible, and refer to the law of 'conservation of energy and matter'. Some physicists refer simply to 'conservation of energy', viewing matter as a type of energy. The concept of energy, as we use it today, was first used by the brilliant thinker Thomas Young. Credit for developing the conservation principle belongs not only to Helmholtz, but also to Joule (1818-1889) and to Mayer (1814-1878).

Helmholtz, a schoolteacher's son, was born in Potsdam, near Berlin. He became a Prussian Army surgeon, and in 1858 was made Professor of Physiology at Königsberg. Later he held the Chair of Anatomy at Heidelberg and of Physics at Berlin, which indicates his wide-ranging skills. As well as major contributions to the theory of physics, he is noted for working out the mechanism of hearing, finding the speeds of nervous impulses and inventing the ophthalmoscope (1850).

See: Entropy, Food Supplies Energy, Interference, Relativity Theories.

Continental Drift (1915)

Alfred Lothar Wegener (1880-1930)

Wegener, a German meteorologist and astronomer, suggested that the continents were once grouped together as 'Pangaea' ('all-earth'), a single enormous piece of granite. This broke up, and the continents drifted apart. For some time the idea was rejected, in spite of much favourable evidence, eg the jigsaw-like fit between the western coast of Africa and the eastern coast of South America. It is now known that the continents lie on tectonic plates, rigid sheets of rock that can move.

Wegener was educated at Heidelberg, Innsbruck and Berlin. When he was fifty he died on an expedition to Greenland, before plate tectonics had become accepted.

Cosmic Rays (1911)

Victor Francis Hess (1883-1964)

Hess, an Austrian physicist, discovered these rays during high-level balloon flights. He used a gold leaf electroscope, a glass box containing two pieces of gold foil attached to a metal rod. If the rod is charged with static electricity, the pieces of foil spring apart. Streams of charged particles or highly energetic radiation produce ions which discharge the pieces of foil, so they come back together. Hess's electroscope showed the presence of penetrating rays, increasing in intensity with height. The rays come in all directions from outer space, and Robert Millikan, a US researcher, gave them their name from cosmos - universe. As they could penetrate even 2 m (6.6 ft) of lead, Millikan thought they were electromagnetic waves of unusually high energy. Arthur Compton, another American, showed they were particles, as they were deflected by the earth's magnetic held. Millikan was dubious still, and Carl Anderson checked that cosmic rays could be bent by a strong field. His experiments led to the discovery of the positron. Cosmic rays are streams of protons and other particles, possessing fantastically high energies. Probably they result from nuclear reactions and are accelerated as they rush through space by cosmic magnetic fields.

Hess was born in Waldstein, Styria. At Graz University he obtained a doctorate in 1906 and a chair in 1920. He spent two years in America, and in 1944 became a US citizen. Because his wife was Jewish, he left Austria before Hitler took it over, staying in Switzerland before settling in New York State.

See: Antimatter, Positron, Proton.

Cullinan Diamond (1905)

M.F. Wells

In January 1905 Captain Maurice Wells, a mine manager, found the world's largest diamond. After a worker reported something sparkling, he prised it out of a wall. He discovered it in the Premier Mine, near Pretoria, South Africa, and named it in honour of the mine's discoverer. It weighed 3106 metric carats, or 621g (11lb 6oz).

The 'Star of Africa' – the largest cut diamond – was cleaved from the Cullinan in 1908. It has 74 facets and a weight of 530 metric carats (106g). Eight other large stones and ninety-six small ones were also cut from the Cullinan.

D

Dark matter (1932)
Jan Hendrix Oort (1900-1992)

The Dutchman Dr Jan Oort was the first astrophysicist to hypothesise the existence of dark matter – invisible interstellar material detectable only by its gravitational effects. Oort was trying to account for the unexpectedly high orbital velocities of stars in our own galaxy, the Milky Way. In 1933 Fritz Zwicky, who was trying to explain the orbital speeds of galaxies in clusters, arrived at the same explanation.

Oort is considered one of the greatest astronomers of the 20th century. He became Professor of Astronomy at the University of Leiden, and for many years he was the director of its observatory. Before going to Leiden he had studied stellar dynamics at the University of Groningen. He made several contributions concerning the dynamics of the Milky Way, establishing that it is rotating in relation to the rest of the universe, and overturned the idea that the Sun is at its centre. He discovered the Galactic Halo, a group of stars orbiting the Milky Way outside the main disc, and was a pioneer in the field of radio astronomy.

Much remains to be learned about dark matter, although it is believed to make up around 26 per cent of the universe by mass, while conventional matter constitutes only 5 per cent – the bulk of the universe, around 69 per cent, appears to consist of the equally mysterious dark energy. Dark matter is thought to consist of a hypothetical sub-atomic particle dubbed the WIMP – weakly interacting massive particle - which does not react to light, neither emitting nor absorbing it.

Oort was born in the town of Franeker in Friesland, the second son of Abraham Hendrikus Oort and his wife Hannah. He married in 1927 and had two sons and a daughter. For a time he worked at Yale University, where he developed an interest in Jules Verne. He died in Leiden at the age of 92. His name is remembered for the Oort Cloud, the region on the outer limits of the solar system from which long-period comets are thought to come.

Dead Sea Scrolls (1946)
Mohammed edh-Dhib (1933-1969)

A Bedouin shepherd boy, Mohammed edh-Dhib found the first scrolls when looking for a straying animal. He saw a hole in a cliff into which he threw a stone which made a strange sound. Climbing into the cave the next day, he found big terracotta jars with lids containing scrolls wrapped in linen. Over the next nine years, another ten caves containing documents were found. The first scrolls were carefully stored, but others seemed to have been dumped hastily immediately before Qumran in Israel was destroyed by the Romans. Qumran was the home of a Jewish sect, probably the Essenes, who largely lived in caves. The scrolls, consisting of biblical and non-biblical documents, were stored between about 150 BC and AD 68, when the Romans destroyed the centre.

Between 1946 and 1956, 981 texts were found; some were in poor condition. They fell into three groups. Group A (40%) had been copied from the Bible, Group B (30%) related to the Second Temple Period and the remaining 30% of Group C are sectarian manuscripts of documents not previously known which refer to various groups within Judaism. In 2014, nine scrolls were rediscovered by the Israel Antiquities Authority; they had been stored unopened for six decades following their excavation in 1952.

These texts have high historical, religious and linguistic significance. Four languages are used, Hebrew, Aramaic, Greek and Nabataean. They are written mainly on parchment, with some on papyrus or bronze. Traditionally the scrolls were associated with the Essenes, an ancient Jewish sect thought to have created them between 408 BC and 318 BC, but it is possible that they were penned by priests in Jerusalem.

Mainstream scholars consider that there is no connection between the scrolls and Jesus Christ. They do show that Christianity is rooted in Judaism, and they have been termed the 'evolutionary link' between the two religions. Some claim that the scrolls were created by a marginal apocalyptic movement and believe that they came from Jewish zealots; these men had much in common with followers of Christ and could have been followers themselves.

Decoding Hieroglyphics (1821)

Jean François Champollion (1790-1832)

In 1799 an officer of Napoleon's army found the Rosetta Stone in Egypt. On the basalt slab were three inscriptions, one in Greek, one in picture writing or 'hieroglyphics' and one in demotic script (a simplified kind of Egyptian writing). Hieroglyphic writing was invented in about 3100 BC. Only the Greek version could he read, but clearly the other inscriptions were translations. Champollion, a French antiquities student, succeeded in cracking the hieroglyphic and the demotic scripts, following his idea that they were related to Coptic, a language still remembered by some Egyptian Christians.

Deuterium (1932)

Harold Urey (1893-1981)

Deuterium or 'heavy hydrogen' is an isotope of ordinary hydrogen (hydrogen-1, in which the nucleus is a bare proton). Deuterium is hydrogen-2, in which the nucleus contains one neutron and one proton:

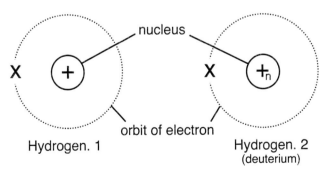

+ = proton, x = electron, n = neutron

ln 1932 Urey discovered deuterium by slow evaporation of a vast amount of water. The few final drops of water gave spectroscopic evidence of heavy hydrogen. Urey named the atom deuterium after the Greek word for 'second'. 'Heavy water' has molecules containing atoms of deuterium. It became famous in the making of the first atomic bomb as a 'moderator' (slower-down) of fast-moving neutrons. Hydrogen also has a rare third isotope, tritium, in which the atom has two neutrons in its nucleus.

Urey was born near Walkerton, Indiana, and graduated in zoology from Montana State University in 1917. His zest for chemical science arose from work with explosives during the First World War. He obtained a PhD in California (1923) and in 1929 joined Colombia University, where he came to achieve pioneering success in separating isotopes.

See: Electron, Isotopes, Neutron, Proton.

Distance of Moon from Earth & Precession of the Equinoxes (c. 150 BC)

Hipparchus of Nicaea (c.190-c.126 BC)

In 250 BC the Greek Aristarchus realised that an eclipse of the Moon is caused by the Earth coming between the Sun and Moon. The curve of the Earth's shadow crossing the Moon showed the relative sizes of Earth and Moon. This enabled the Earth-Moon distance to be estimated. Hipparchus repeated the work of Aristarchus, to find that the distance is thirty limes the Earth's diameter. Using Eratosthenes' value for the latter gave a good result for the Earth-Moon distance (386,401 km or about 240,000 miles).

The Earth bulges at the Equator, and the varying pull of the

Moon on the bulge makes the Earth's axis of rotation mark out a double cone. This means each pole points to a steadily-changing point in the sky. The points form a circle, around which a pole revolves every twenty-six thousand years. Hipparchus noted the shift, which makes the sun get to the point of equinox fifty seconds of arc eastwards each year, in the direction of morning. As the equinox comes annually to an earlier point, Hipparchus named the shift the 'precession of the equinoxes'.

See: Earth's Circumference and Diameter.

DNA and RNA (1911)
Phoebus Aaron Theodore Levene (1869-1940)

In 1869 F. Miescher in Switzerland showed that the nucleus of a cell contains a substance later named 'nucleic acid'. A few years later the German Albrecht Kossel found this contains four nitrogen-containing compounds, adenine, guanine, cytosine and thymine, and he also found a carbohydrate. Levene, a pupil of Kossel, discovered in 1911 that there are two distinct nucleic acids. One, RNA or ribonucleic acid, contains the sugar ribose. The other, DNA or deoxyribonucleic acid, contains deoxyribose, a sugar similar to ribose, but with one oxygen atom less. RNA was also found to differ from DNA in containing not thymine but uracil, a similar substance.

By 1934 Levene's researches showed that DNA and RNA are built up of nucleotides, as a protein is built up of amino acids. A nucleotide contains a sugar (ribose or deoxyribose), a purine (adenine or guanine) or a pyrimidine (cytosine, thymine or uracil) and a phosphate group. In 1944 it was shown that DNA is what genes are made of. The genetic coding is given in any one particular region of a chromosome by the precise arrangement of the purine and pyrimidine. RNA is the messenger-compound which carries the code, imprinted on its nucleotide network, to the cytoplasm, the part of the cell outside the nucleus. In the cytoplasm are biological catalysts or 'enzymes' that cause amino acids and proteins to he made as 'instructed' by RNA. In some viruses, 'retroviruses', only RNA is present and this carries out both functions.

Levene carried out all his research in the United States, although he was born in Sagar, Russia. In 1873 his family moved to St Petersburg, and in 1891 they emigrated to America. Levene returned to Russia to finish reading medicine, and settled in the USA in 1892. After studying chemistry at Colombia University he abandoned medicine for biochemistry.

See: Cell Division, Structure of Nucleic Acids.

Helical structure of DNA and RNA

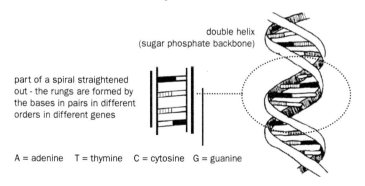

double helix
(sugar phosphate backbone)

part of a spiral straightened out - the rungs are formed by the bases in pairs in different orders in different genes

A = adenine   T = thymine   C = cytosine   G = guanine

The backbone is a double helix running the length of the molecule. It is like a twisted ladder. The rungs are pairs of bases, either adenine linked with thymine or cytosine linked with guanine. The order in which the bases are arranged is variable; it forms a genetic code containing instructions for developing such things as the colour of our eyes, shape of our nose etc.

Dolomitic Rock (1781)

Déodat Guy Gratet de Dolomieu (1750-1801)

This French army officer became a professor of mineralogy. He studied the origin and composition of igneous rocks by comparing them with the products of volcanoes. Sulphur, he thought, caused volcanic eruptions and the viscosity of a rock, resulting in its glassy or crystalline structure. His chemical analysis of limestones of the South Tyrol showed a high content of magnesium. Ever since, both that region of Austria and similar limestones in other regions have been named 'Dolomites' after him.

Doppler Effect (1842)

Christian Johann Doppler (1803-1853)

In 1842 Doppler, an Austrian physicist, discovered the wave effect named after him. We all experience it with sound; the siren of a police car, for instance, becomes higher as the car comes towards us, then drops in pitch as it moves away. The pitch changes because the car's motion towards or away from the observer changes the number of sound waves reaching the ear each second. In 1842 Doppler deduced a mathematical relationship between pitch and relative movement between the source of sound and the observer. Two years later the relationship was proved in a weird experiment in which a locomotive carrying trumpeters went to and fro past stationary observers, professional musicians who could record the pitch of the notes heard.

With light, the shift is in frequency. If a source of light is approaching, more waves are crowded into each second and the light seen shifts toward the violet (high frequency) end of the spectrum. If the source is moving away, the shift is towards the red (low frequency) end. In 1912 the American Vesto Slipher found such a 'red shift' in the light from distant stars. In a revolutionary discovery in the 1920s, Edwin Hubble used the effect to show that all the galaxies are rushing away from one another, and that hence the universe is expanding.

Doppler was born in Salzburg, the son of a master mason. He gave up a plan to move to America when offered a professorship at a school in Prague in 1835. Subsequently, he held a chair at Prague Technical College and in Chemnitz, Germany. ln 1850 he became Professor of Experimental Physics in Vienna, but died only three years later in Italy.

See: Big Bang, Expanding Universe.

Down's Syndrome (1866)

John Langdon Haydon Down (1828-1896)

John Langdon Down, an English physician, first described this disease, once called 'mongolism', as one of its symptoms is a slant of the eyelids giving an appearance somewhat like that of Asian or Mongolian people. The syndrome occurs once in every thousand births and involves mild to moderate intellectual disability. ln 1959, three French geneticists found that the cause is one chromosome too many; chromosome pair 21 has three chromosomes, instead of two. Amniocentesis makes it possible to discover in early pregnancy whether or not a foetus has Down's syndrome.

In 1866 Down published a paper based on his studies at the

Earlsfield Hospital, Wimbledon, in *London Hospital Reports*. The paper put mental patients in five classes - Caucasian, Ethiopian, Malay, American and Mongolian. Particular attention was given to the last group, and Down's name became associated with the term 'mongol', now rejected. He was not a racist but a compassionate and much-respected physician who committed himself to aiding patients in asylums. In his time this was most unusual.

Earth is a Magnet (1600)
William Gilbert (1544-1603)

Gilbert was court physician to Queen Elizabeth l and King James l of England. He achieved fame for *De Magnete*, a classic treatise on magnetism. One of his experiments described a magnetised needle suspended so it could pivot vertically. Its north pole dipped toward the ground. He obtained the same result using a ball of lodestone as a model Earth and a small needle. Gilbert could not explain his findings. Today the Earth's magnetism and its variations are thought to be due to the motion of molten iron in the outer core.

Earth is Spherical (525 BC)
Pythagoras of Samos (c. 580-500 BC)

Credit for being first to recognise that the Earth is spherical is generally given to Pythagoras. He was not the first person to put forward what became known as Pythagoras' Theorem, but he did prove it to be true. Aristotle had said that the Earth is a ball because of the shape of its shadow on the Moon during an eclipse of the Moon. The ancient Greeks had various other reasons for accepting this concept, such as the fact that when a ship appeared over the horizon its sails were always seen before the hull. The concept of a flat Earth tended to prevail after the Greeks, but even during the Dark Ages the idea of the Earth as a ball never died completely.

Earth's Circumference and Diameter (240 BC)
Eratosthenes of Cyrene (c.276-c.194 BC)

Eratosthenes was put in charge of the museum at Alexandria, Egypt, the greatest scientific institution of that time. Around 240 BC he observed that, at noon on 21st June, the sun was directly overhead at Syene, five hundred miles south of Alexandria, but not quite at its zenith at Alexandria. By finding a shadow's length in Alexandria at zenith at noon, he deduced the curvature of the Earth from Syene to Alexandria. Taking the planet as a giant ball, he used his results to obtain these values in modern units:

$$\text{Circumference} = 40{,}250 \text{ km } (25{,}000 \text{ miles})$$
$$\text{Diameter} = 12{,}880 \text{ km } (8000 \text{ miles})$$

These very good values were largely ignored, and the favoured results were smaller values obtained in 100 BC by the Greek Posidonius. The latter's figures led Columbus to envisage that a voyage of only 4830 km (3000 miles) would take him from Europe to Asia. In 1521-1523 the circumnavigation by the remaining ship of Magellan's fleet showed that Eratosthenes' results had been correct.

See: America from Spain.

Easter Island from the Netherlands (1722)

Jacob Roggeveen (1659-1729)

A Dutch admiral, Roggeveen was the first European to visit this remote isle in the south-eastern Pacific. He named it after the Sunday he landed - Easter Day, 1722. Keen to explore further, he was not particularly interested in the dark-skinned Polynesian inhabitants or in the giant statues scattered across the island. The statues are thought to have been carved and positioned by the islanders some 500-700 years ago. There are over one thousand, some 9.5m (32 ft) tall and weighing 90 tonnes. Probably they represent spiritual leaders or chiefs of Polynesians who arrived from the west around the year zero. Admiral Roggeveen discovered no other islands. Later, the Dutch East India Company confiscated his vessels on the grounds that he was infringing its monopoly.

See: Pacific Islands from England.

Echo-sounding by Bats (1770)

Lazaro Spallanzani (1729-1799)

This Italian abbot and naturalist heard it rumoured that blind bats could fly without difficulty. Together with a Swiss, Louis Jurine, he covered bats' ears and found they flew wildly, hitting objects and each other, although their eyes were not covered. He also blinded bats, and found they could still fly and catch insects. They made no noise but he deduced bats use sounds of some kind to navigate in the dark, the waves being reflected from obstacles. In 1920 it was suggested that bats navigate using the reflection of high-pitched ultrasonic squeals, and experiments in 1938 confirmed this theory.

In 1765 Spallanzani showed that broth in open vessels soon teemed with micro-organisms, but boiled and sealed-up broth stayed sterile. He concluded that 'spontaneous generation' of life from inanimate matter was impossible, but this was not accepted until work by Louis Pasteur ninety-seven years later. In 1779 Spallanzani proved that semen is necessary for fertilisation.

Spallanzani was born in Scandiano, Modena, and died in Pavia, Lombardy. He studied at Bologna University, where a female cousin was Professor of Physics. He became a priest to survive, as his real love was biological research.

See: Ultrasonics.

Edison Effect (1883)

Thomas Alva Edison (1847-1931)

Edison, the renowned American inventor, made one discovery of note, in 1883. He sealed a metal wire into a light bulb close to the hot filament, and was surprised to discover that a current flowed across the gap from the filament to the wire. In 1904 the Englishman John Fleming utilised this 'Edison effect' to invent the diode valve. Edison himself recorded his discovery, but is not thought to have tried to make use of it.

Electric Cell (1800)

Count Alessandro Giuseppe Antonio Anastasio Volta (1745-1827)

Volta, an Italian physicist, reported his discovery of the electric cell in 1800. He had been studying combinations of metals connected by simple solutions. His 'voltaic pile' was a stack of alternate copper and zinc discs, separated by discs of cardboard wetted with salty water. It was a forerunner of the modern torch battery. Volta was friendly with Galvani, but realised Galvani's discovery of 'animal electricity' did not hold water.

He was one of nine children, and spent much of his life in Como. He was born there, went to school there, taught physics there and his life ended there. In 1779 he became a professor at Pavia, and in 1801 Napoleon called him to Paris to demonstrate his experiments. His name lives on in the voltameter, the voltmeter and of course the volt, the unit of electromotive force.

Electric Current (1791)

Luigi Galvani (1737-1798)

The Italian anatomist Galvani accidentally discovered 'animal electricity'. He found that if thigh muscles from dissected frogs were touched by two different metals, they contracted. This also happened if the muscles were stimulated by a spark from a Leyden jar, and Galvani thought the muscle tissue was necessary. He misunderstood what he saw, but is remembered for being the first to show the existence of moving electric charge. His name survives in science, as in 'galvanometer' and 'galvanised iron', but also in the verb to 'galvanise' into action.

In early life he studied theology, but then changed to medicine. In 1762 he became a lecturer at Bologna University, and in 1775 he took over the chair of anatomy there. His life ended on a down note. In 1797 his university post was taken away because he had declined to swear allegiance to a new government authorised by Napoleon Bonaparte.

See: Electric Cell.

Electroconvulsive Therapy (ECT) (1938)

Ugo Cerletti (1902-1987)

Shock treatment for mental illness or severe depression was first tried with drugs, eg the use of an insulin overdose to treat schizophrenia. The attempts were dangerous, and often quickly abandoned, eg. camphor produced convulsions which were violent enough to break bones. In 1938 Cerletti and Lucio Bini discovered the value of treatment by electric shocks. The value of ECT is debatable, but it is still in use in some countries for treating very depressed patients. The original procedure produced a convulsion, while today a muscle relaxant is given to suppress this reaction. A patient, while lightly anaesthetised, has a small current applied to the scalp.

Electromagnetic Induction (1831) and Laws of Electrolysis (1832)

Michael Faraday (1791-1867)

Faraday was horn in Newington Butts, a Surrey village. Soon the family moved to North London. Money was short; when he was ten, Faraday's diet was mainly bread, and two years later he had to work. When he was fourteen he became an apprentice bookbinder, which led to an interest in reading, especially about science. He joined a scientific society, and in 1812 went to hear Davy lecture at the Royal Institution. When Davy was blinded in an explosion, he acted as a temporary secretary for him. Subsequently he was taken on as laboratory assistant, and in 1813 he accompanied Davy and his new wife on an eighteen–month tour of Europe. On his return he soon became a scientific consultant at the Royal Institution.

Faraday and Davy both had an interest in chemistry and in electricity. However, Davy grew very jealous of his brilliant protégé, and initially opposed his election to the Royal Society in the early 1820s.

In 1823 Faraday found how to liquefy chlorine gas and in 1825 be discovered benzene. Seven years later he proposed the two laws of electrolysis, which concern chemical changes brought about by electricity. Significant as his chemical discoveries were, he is most remembered for his 1831 discovery of electromagnetic induction. He found that a voltage is induced in a conductor if the number of magnetic lines of force passing through it changes, and a current flows if the conductor is part of a circuit. He invented the transformer and discovered the basis of the electric motor (which turns current into rotation) and the dynamo (which turns rotation into current). His concept of the space between magnetic or electric objects being filled with 'force fields', represented by 'lines of force', was of great significance. He did for electromagnetism what Einstein was to do for gravitation. In 1832 he deposited a sealed envelope at the Royal Society. When opened one hundred and seven years later, it was found to contain the suggestion that there exist electromagnetic waves, comparable to water waves.

Faraday belonged to a Protestant sect, the Sandemanians. In 1821 he married Sarah Barnard, a sect member. The couple were childless, but in 1827 Faraday inaugurated the Royal Institution Christmas science lectures for children. These continue today, and are televised. In 1841 Faraday became very ill, and never recovered fully. He died at Hampton Court near London in a house that Queen Victoria had provided for him.

See: Alkali Metals and Alkaline-Earth Metals, Benzene Ring, Electromagnetic Waves.

Electromagnetic Waves (1865)

James Clerk Maxwell (1831-1879)

This Scottish theoretical physicist predicted the existence of these waves, consisting of electrical and magnetic disturbances. Following Faraday's introduction of 'field theory' and 'lines of force', Maxwell expressed this approach in mathematical terms. In 1864 he developed four equations which showed an electric field cannot be separated from a magnetic field, and changing it will produce waves propagating out in all directions. This led him to produce his famous *Treatise on Electricity and Magnetism* (1873), in which light is said to be electromagnetic vibrations. Faraday himself had actually privately reached this conclusion in 1832.

Maxwell suggested that visible light is one portion of a family of these radiations. Definite confirmation of this came eight years after his death, with Hertz's production of radio waves when generating an oscillating current from the spark of an induction coil. Soon the existence of a spectrum of electromagnetic waves was established. The highest frequencies, smallest wavelengths and highest penetrating powers belong to y- (gamma) rays:

NAME OF RAYS	DISCOVERED BY	COUNTRY	YEAR
γ (gamma)	Paul Villard	France	1900
X	Wilhelm Röntgen	Germany	1895
ultra Violet	Johann Ritter	Germany	1801
light			
infra-red	William Hershel	England	1800
microwave	Karl Jansky	USA	1931
radio wave	Heinrich Hertz	Germany	1887

Light rays represent only a small part of the electromagnetic spectrum, from extreme violet (wavelength (0.39 microns) to extreme red (wavelength 0.78 microns). (1 micron = 1 millionth of a metre.) If, as with sound waves, we take a doubling of wavelength as a range of 1 octave, the full range is 60 octaves, while visible light covers 1 octave. The band of waves used in broadcasting covers about 1 1/3 octaves. Although electromagnetic waves have a variety of frequencies and wavelengths, they have the same velocity (297,600 km/sec or 186,000 miles/sec in a vacuum). In his special theory of relativity, Einstein suggested that this is the highest speed possible and has the same value for all observers.

Maxwell, an only son, was born in Edinburgh. His mother passed away when he was nine. He entered Cambridge in 1850, and became a professor at Aberdeen six years later. A brilliant mathematician, he worked out, with Ludwig Boltzmann, the kinetic energy of gases (1860). This explained the behaviour of gases in terms of continuously moving molecules. It was significant in showing heat to be the equivalent to molecular motion (as Rumford had suggested in 1798) and in reinforcing the concept of the 'molecule', which some found hard to accept. Maxwell said he found it helpful to clarity his scientific thinking by holding imaginary conversations with his dog.

In 1871 he took up the Cambridge chair of experimental physics. He published Henry Cavendish's impressive findings in electricity, which Cavendish himself had not released. It was through Maxwell that the famous Cavendish Research Laboratory was set up. His premature death at forty-eight was due to cancer.

See: Electromagnetic Induction and Laws of Electrolysis, Gravitation, Laws of Motion and Dispersion of White Light, Heat is a Vibration, Hydrogen, Relativity Theories, Wave Theory of Light, X-Rays.

Electromagnetism (1820)
Hans Christian Oersted (1777-1851)

Oersted, a Danish physicist, was the discoverer of the magnetic effect of electric current. When a current flowed along a wire it deflected a compass needle placed nearby. The deflection was at 90° to the wire-compass direction, indicating that the current's magnetic force acted in circles around the wire. Oersted's surprising discovery stimulated Faraday to find ways of converting electricity into movement.

Oersted's younger brother became Prime Minister of Denmark. Their birthplace was Rudkøbing, Langeland. Their father owned an apothecary's business, but it was to physics that the young Oersted was drawn. At Copenhagen University he obtained a doctorate in 1799, and seven years later the chair of physics and chemistry. He was actually teaching when he made his profound discovery in 1820, and stayed on when the students departed, fascinated by what he saw. In the same year he was the first to isolate piperidine, an organic compound, while in 1825 he was the first to isolate aluminium.

See: Electromagnetic Induction and Laws of Electrolysis.

Electron (1897)
Sir Joseph John Thomson (1856-1940)

In 1876 the German Eugen Goldstein thought that cathode rays were electromagnetic radiation. The English physicist William Crookes showed that they are probably streams of charged particles, as they are deflected by a magnet. Then Thomson established in

1897 that cathode rays are also deflected by electric charges and must contain negatively-charged particles. The only such particles then known were negative ions, which were deflected much less than cathode rays. Thomson's work led to a general acceptance that the electron is an extraordinarily light particle, and the unit of negative electricity.

A much harder pill to swallow was the news that atoms contain electrons. This contradicted the view of Democritus and Dalton that atoms were indivisible. However, Thomson showed that the negatively-charged particles produced by the photoelectric effect are the same as the particles in cathode rays. Other discoveries, such as the Edison effect, suggested electrons were particles found in every atom.

As electrons are easily removed from atoms, it was concluded that they are on the outside. In 1913 Niels Bohr, a Danish physicist, suggested that the atom resembles a minute solar system with, at its centre, a positively-charged nucleus. Circling the nucleus in definite orbits were electrons, rather like planets around the sun. Bohr's scheme, which won him the 1922 Nobel Prize for Physics, became increasingly complex. In 1926 the German Erwin Schrodinger worked out 'wave mechanics', a mathematical description of the atom in which electrons were treated not as particles but as waves. Today we accept the electron as having properties of both particles and waves. Planck's quantum theory (1900) was of great value in our understanding the behaviour of the electron and other so-called 'particles'.

Thomson was born near Manchester and entered college at the age of fourteen. In 1876 he obtained a scholarship to Cambridge, where he stayed. When he was twenty-seven he was made a professor of physics and in 1906 he was given the Nobel Prize for Physics. This was also won by seven people who had worked under 'JJ', including Lord Rutherford.

See: Atom, Atomic Theory, Cathode and Channel Rays, Edison Effect, Photoelectric Effect, Positron, Proton.

Elements (1661) and Boyle's Law (1662)

Robert Boyle (1627-1691)

Boyle, 'the father of chemistry', published in his *Sceptical Chymist* (1661) the modern concept of a chemical element. He laid down the criterion that an element cannot be broken down into any simpler substance. Today we know that while this is possible, it cannot be done by ordinary chemical methods. In Boyle's time, there was confusion about which substances are elements; eg lime (calcium oxide) and salt (sodium chloride) were viewed as elements, while gold and arsenic were not.

In 1662 Boyle experimented with air and deduced the law named after him, which connects the volume of a gas with the pressure on it. His work was the first in a series of discoveries about matter that culminated in the atomic theory. In earlier experiments, Boyle showed that light and heavy objects fall at equal rates in a vacuum, that the human body has a steady temperature, higher than the air around it, and that burning has similarities to respiration.

Boyle was born at Lismore Castle, Ireland, the fourteenth child of the Earl of Cork. He became an infant prodigy, and when at eight he went to Eton he was already proficient in Latin and Greek. At eleven he travelled through Europe. When in Geneva he became a devout Christian because of a violent thunderstorm. His medical books (1684-1691) emphasised the scientific aspects of medicine. Much of his life was spent in London, where he died.

See: Atom, Atomic Theory.

Entropy (1850)

Rudolf Julius Emanuel Clausius (1822-1888)

Thermodynamics, which studies the transfer of energy from one body to another, is based on four laws concerned particularly with heat transfer. These laws relate to

Clausius's concept of entropy or the amount of disorder in any physical system. It measures how much useful energy ('work' in physics) can be obtained from a system. Energy can be extracted only by entropy increase. Think of a hot poultice applied to an inflamed ankle. After some time, the poultice and skin will be at the same temperature, and it is not possible to obtain any more useful energy from the poultice. There is no possibility of recapturing the dissipated heat energy.

The same principle applies to the universe, ie its degree of disorder tends to increase and can never decrease. It has been said that eventually the 'heat death' of the universe will come, in which energy is eventually distributed everywhere and entropy is at a maximum. The amount of usable energy, provided mainly by the stars, is however enormous.

Clausius was born in Köslin, Pomerania, and became a PhD at Halle (1848). By 1869 he was Physics Professor at Bonn, and kept this position for the rest of his working life.

See: Absolute Zero.

Escapology (1897)

Harry Houdini (1874-1926)

The most expert of all escape artists was born Erich Weiss in Hungary. He was the son of a rabbi, and emigrated to America when a young man. A showman all his life, he began as a magician and called himself Houdini after an illustrious predecessor. Enthusiasm for escapology came with a discovery that he could escape from handcuffs by making his wrists swell temporarily when the cuffs were put on.

As his escapes became more and more baffling, audiences flocked to see him perform. Some involved pure trickery, as with his escaping from a water-filled barrel. However, he trained himself to get out of leg-irons and straitjackets, and he also became prolific in escape techniques such as picking locks. He pioneered underwater escapes from roped and locked boxes, inside which he was seen to be handcuffed and shackled. In the USA and Europe he escaped – sometimes unclothed – from cells the police had declared 'totally secure'. One such cell was at Scotland Yard, London.

An interest in communicating with the dead led him to investigate mediums. All proved unconvincing or were using trickery, a field not unknown to Houdini. He promised that after dying, he would do his best to send his wife some signal on his birthday. For several years she waited with friends on the day, but this was a trick not even he could manage.

His death at fifty-two was a tragedy. While lying on a couch recovering from a broken ankle, he apparently told a reporter he was so fit that he could withstand being punched in the stomach. Without giving Houdini a chance to brace himself, the reporter hit him so hard that the blow caused internal damage, and Houdini died of acute appendicitis soon afterwards.

Expanding Universe (1924)

Edwin Hubble (1889-1953)

In 1924, Hubble showed that the Milky Way is just one galaxy among a vast number in the universe. He proved, from the faintness of the stars in them, that the so-called 'spiral nebulae' are distant clusters of stars, or galaxies, in their own right. Then in 1929 came Hubble's law, which stated that the galaxies are moving apart at speeds which increase in proportion to distance.

Hubble started out studying law but, gaining interest in astronomy, became an observer at Mount Wilson, California, USA. His extremely significant findings had actually been predicted in 1922 by Alexander Friedmann. This Russian mathematician showed that we should not expect the universe to be static, as Einstein and many others did. His views stemmed from an assumption that wherever we look, the universe appears identical, and that this is true for any observer anywhere in the universe. The news that the galaxies were rushing away from one another led to the 'big bang' concept of the universe, first suggested in 1927.

A light year is the distance light travels in one year – is about 9.65 x 10^{12} (9,650,000,000,000) km or 6 x 10^{12} (6,000,000,000,000) miles.

Hubble was once visited at Mount Wilson Observatory by Einstein and wife Elsa. An assistant showed them the giant telescope, and remarked that it was useful in working out the structure of the cosmos. 'Well,' said Elsa, 'my husband does that on the backs of old envelopes'.

RESULTS OF SOME US EXPERIMENTS VERIFYING HUBBLE'S LAW FOR GALAXIES DISTANT FROM THE MILKY WAY★

Cluster nebula in:	Distance from Earth in light years	Speed of recession Kms/sec	miles/sec
Virgo	65,000,000	1,207	750
Ursa Major	100,000,000	15,000	9,300
Corona Borealis	130,000,000	22,600	13,400
Bootes	230,000,000	39,260	24,400
Hydra	350,000,000	61,142	38,000

★Based on information published by the California Institute of Technology (1981)

Newton, and even Einstein, took it for granted that the universe is static. Hubble showed that the galaxies are flying apart, and the more distant a galaxy is from us, the higher its velocity. Today it is recognised that it is clusters of galaxies that are travelling away from each other. The expansion stretches the light waves from distant objects towards the long wavelength - red - part of the spectrum, making the light 'red-shifted'. The extent of the shift is directly proportional to an object's distance, and red shifts enable the distances to the more remote objects in the universe to be measured. The red shift of galaxies is similar to the Doppler effect. (p.70).
See: Big Bang, Relativity Theories.

Food As A Source Of Energy (1842)
Julius Robert von Mayer (1814-1878)

Von Mayer, a German physician, discovered that chemical energy supports life. When he was a young man he became a surgeon on a Dutch ship voyaging to Java. He was not kept busy and had time to note that the crew ate much more food in the North Sea than in the Indian Ocean, although their daily duties did not alter. The officers, he noticed, ate less than the sailors. Soon after the end of the voyage he realised that food gives us energy, for activity and internal processes and to keep warm. With his appreciation of energy balance, he later assisted in pioneering the law of conservation of energy.

At the time this work received no appreciation and von Mayer gradually became very depressed. ln 1848 two of his children died, and the next year he attempted suicide. This left him lame, but he lived on a further twenty-nine years, until he died at his birthplace, Heilbronn, near Stuttgart.

See: Conservation of Energy.

Fractional Dimensionality (1958)
Benoit Mandelbrot (1924-2010)

A brilliant mathematician, Mandelbrot came to see the similarity of problems in economics, engineering, physiology, physics and other disciplines. He demonstrated, by his concept of fractional dimensionality, how in many contexts superficial order can be correlated with underlying chaos. Born in Poland, he moved to France to escape the Nazi regime. He became a French citizen, but ended up as a research scientist in the USA.

Fraunhofer Lines (1814)
Joseph von Fraunhofer (1787-1826)

In 1814 this German optician passed sunlight through a slit and into a prism, which he had made so precisely that the spectrum it produced showed dark lines where light of that exact wavelength was absent. He mapped the lines, which were soon named after their discoverer. More than 700 were recorded by Fraunhofer, while with modern instruments, more than 30,000 have been found. Only after Fraunhofer's death was it realised that the spectral lines represent absorption of light at particular wavelengths by different elements. Bright lines represent characteristic emissions of light by elements. Spectroscopy utilises the lines as 'fingerprints' to show which elements are present in light from a particular source. The technique led to the discovery of helium in the Sun (1868), and has been immensely valuable in chemistry and astronomy.

Fraunhofer, the son of a glazier, was born in Straubing, Bavaria.

When he was eleven, his tenement home collapsed, killing his family and leaving him the sole survivor. His glass-making skills became very advanced, and it was this that resulted in his discovery, He died at thirty-nine in M nich, of tuberculosis.

See: Helium.

G

Gaia Theory (1979)
James Lovelock (1919-)

Gaia was the Greek goddess of the Earth. Lovelock, an English environmentalist, said conservation maintained the totality of the planet's existence. He said the chemical and physical conditions of the surface, oceans and atmosphere were kept in good order by living things. Conventionally it is held that life adapts to Earth conditions, so the idea that our planet could be a self-regulating entity was a radical departure from conventional theory. Lovelock is an independent scientist and inventor who has contributed to NASA's programme of exploring planets. The electron capture detector – one of several devices he invented – revealed the worldwide distribution of pesticide residues.

Gaulois Theory (1830)
Evariste Gaulois (1811-1832)

This theory brings together several branches of mathematics, aiding the study of important problems. It can be employed in topics as diverse as solving a sextic equation (eg. $X^6 + 2x^5 - 5x^4 + 9x^3 - 5x^2 + 2x + 1 = 0$) and proving the impossibility of squaring the circle (constructing a square which has the same area as a given circle).

Gaulois was born near Paris, and started at high school in 1823. By the age of fifteen he was reading books written for professional mathematicians. In 1829 his father killed himself following a political dispute. Gaulois soon made major discoveries in the theory of polynomial equations. With any polynomial, he associated a group of permutations of its zeros (the 'Gaulois group'). He submitted his results to the Academy of Sciences, but no attention was paid to them. In 1831 he was imprisoned for six months for leading a Republican demonstration wearing the uniform of a disbanded organisation. The next year he was wounded in a duel and died within hours of peritonitis.

Germ Theory of Disease (1840)
Friedrich Gustav Jakob Henle (1809-1885)

Henle, a German pathologist, initiated this theory. Realising that certain animal diseases were due to infections by fungi, he suggested that the causes of many diseases were living parasites or 'germs' which 'germinated' in their hosts. Henle's ideas were put to practical use by a student of his, Robert Koch, in 1881, when investigating tuberculosis. By finding ways of preparing pure solid cultures, Koch was able to discover the causes of TB and other diseases. Louis Pasteur developed a similar technique in his work on pathogenic micro-organisms. His work with cultures used sugar solutions and other liquids as media, and was less successful than Koch's. Pasteur's main contribution to the germ theory came from his investigations into malfunctions of brewing and winemaking.

See: Bacteriological Techniques.

Glacial Flow (1840)

Jean Louis Rodolphe Agassiz (1807-1873)

Agassiz showed that glaciers move by observing lines of stakes he had driven into Alpine glaciers. By 1840 he had found that they flow at a rate of around 67m (225 ft) a year. Many of his investigations were in the central Alps, but he also found evidence of past glaciation in England, France and America. He was a Swiss zoologist and palaeontologist, famous in his lifetime for his classification of fish. In 1846 he went to the USA, and became a professor at Harvard. He is remembered particularly for believing that most of the Earth's surface had once been covered with ice. In fact, he supported the idea of total coverage, with life later being recreated by the Almighty.

Gravitation (1687), Laws of Motion (1687) & Dispersion of White Light (1704)

Sir Isaac Newton (1642-1727)

Newton was born on Christmas Day 1642 at Woolsthorpe, Lincolnshire. He was brought up mainly by his grandmother, and entered Cambridge University when he was nineteen. In 1665 Cambridge was visited by the plague, so he moved back home and spent eighteen months there. During this period he made intense studies of problems relating to calculus, gravitation and light. Rumour has it that an apple falling on his head inspired his explanation of why things fall. In reality, he simply pondered why a dropped apple falls. At Cambridge his reputation grew steadily, and in 1669 he became Professor of Mathematics.

In 1687 he published three volumes of his *Mathematical Principles of Natural Philosophy*. Book 1 explained his laws of motion – three basic 'rules' governing how things move. In the same volume was the theory of universal gravitation: every object attracts every other object. Because of gravitation, the Sun attracts the Earth, the Earth attracts the Moon, the Moon produces tides by attracting the oceans and dropped objects are attracted to the Earth. To an extent Newton anticipated Einstein's theories of relativity in wondering whether motion is absolute or relative (has to be measured in relation to something). In his Book II, he built up a picture of the universe, demolishing much dogma, such as the Roman Catholic insistence on the Earth being stationary. His third book examined predictions that could be made from his ideas. One was that a planet bulges at its equator because it is spinning, and another dealt with the highly elongated orbits of comets.

Opticks, his second main book, appeared in 1704. It explained how a glass prism can disperse sunlight – it splits up white light into the colours of the rainbow, which itself is formed by dispersion. Newton invented the reflecting telescope, and suggested light consists of tiny particles, though today we do not accept the term 'particles' in the way he used it.

In a book on mathematics, he developed the binomial theorem and invented calculus (a method of calculation for continuously altering quantities). A few years later the German Gottfried Leibniz (I646-1716) independently developed calculus, but Newton had published his work later than Leibniz. He reacted with fury when some people thought Leibniz had been first. In fact, much of his later life saw him involved in bitter disputes with other academics.

In 1696 he was appointed Warden of the Royal Mint, where

he became active in revising the coinage and fighting counterfeiting. A few years later he became President of the Royal Society. His knighthood in 1705 was given for his political services, not his prestigious scientific work.

See: Halley's Comet, Jupiter's Satellites and the Law of Falling Bodies, Relativity Theories, Wave Theory of Light.

Greenland from Iceland (983)

Erik the Red (940-1010)

The Norseman Erik Thorvaldsson was dubbed 'red' because of his bright red hair. In 982 AD he was expelled from a Viking colony on Iceland. Sailing west, he came to Greenland, which Irish monks may well have found a century before. Most of the island is covered permanently with ice, but Thorvaldsson selected a name to make it sound attractive. Surprisingly, his ploy worked. In 986 25 ships carrying emigrants left with him for the 'green land'. Only fourteen of them arrived safely. The colonisers founded a settlement in south-west Greenland which survived until the thirteenth century. In 1921 the entire island became the property of Denmark.

See: America from Iceland.

Halley's Comet (1682)
Sir Edmond Halley (1656-1742)

Halley was an English astronomer who took up Newton's ideas about comets. He found that a comet he observed in 1682 was following a similar path to comets seen in 1531 and 1607, which led him to suggest that the three sightings were of the same comet, orbiting the sun about every seventy-six years. In 1758 the comet was sighted again, as Halley had predicted, though he had died sixteen years previously. Successive appearances have since been traced back to 467 BC; the last sighting was in 1986.

Halley calculated his comet's orbit in 1705, and the reappearing body was named after him. Early sightings, like one just before the Battle of Hastings (1066), were regarded as omens of either bad or good fortune. In 1456 the Pope condemned the object as an agent of the devil.

Halley studied at Oxford, and left university to set up the first observatory in the Southern Hemisphere, on St Helena in the South Atlantic. In 1678 he was elected a Fellow of the Royal Society. Six years later he visited his great friend Isaac Newton, who astonished him by stating that he could explain the planetary orbits. A short paper by Newton about this eventually grew into the famous Principia. The drive for this came from Halley, who paid for the printing and did the proofreading. The first edition, in Latin, was published in 1687, mainly at Halley's expense.

In 1703 he was made Professor of Geometry at Oxford, while from 1721 until his death he was Astronomer Royal. This post was concerned particularly with finding a ship's position at sea, which had interested him for some years. He prepared the first detailed mortality tables. He was happily married for fifty-five years and had three children.

See: Gravitation, Laws of Motion and Dispersion of White Light, Laws of Planetary Motion.

Heat is a Vibration (1798)

Count Rumford (Benjamin Thompson) (1753-1814)

When in Bavaria, Germany, in 1798, this American adventurer was supervising the boring of cannons, and was intrigued by the heat generated. It took less than three hours to bring 8kg (18lbs) of water to the boiling point. His conclusion was that heat is a form of vibration, and not matter, as many then thought. The temperature rose as a direct result of the friction of the borer against a cannon. The following year the same conclusion about heat was provided by the Englishman Humphry Davy, who demonstrated that ice can be melted by friction alone.

The American, born Benjamin Thompson, left his country when the revolution began. He acquired the pseudo-title of Count Rumford, and travelled and worked in Western Europe. He was the inventor of the cooking-range and the coffee percolator.

See: Conservation of Energy.

Helium (1868)

Sir Norman Lockyer (1836-1920)

The second simplest element was discovered via sunlight over thirty years before it was found on Earth. The invention in 1859 of the spectroscope allowed elements to be identified by characteristic emissions of light. Soon the procedure was applied to light from the stars. In 1868 a Frenchman, Pierre César, was in India observing a total eclipse of the Sun when he found a spectral line that corresponded to no known element. Lockyer, an English astronomer, decided the line came from a new element and named it from 'helios' (sun).

In 1895, a Scottish chemist, Sir William Ramsey (1852-1916), discovered helium in the atmosphere. Ramsey was the discoverer of other inert gases in air - neon, krypton and xenon. Argon, the inert gas present in the highest proportion (9600 parts per million), was discovered jointly by Ramsey and an English physicist, Lord Rayleigh. Air contains only four parts per million of helium, which seeps from certain natural gas wells. It is the only substance that cannot be solidified at normal pressure. To avoid the 'bends', a diver may breathe an oxygen-helium mixture (instead of air). Such a person temporarily then speaks in a high-pitched squeak.

Lockyer grew up in Rugby, and in 1857 he began work as a War Office clerk. His main hobby - astronomy - soon became his profession. He was the first to investigate the spectra of sunspots. His knighthood came in 1897, following the discovery of helium in air.

See: Fraunhofer Lines, Superconductivity, Superfluidity.

Hilbert Spaces (1904)

David Hilbert (1862-1943)

David Hilbert was a German mathematician of outstanding influence in various branches of the subject. In 1900 he produced a list of twenty-three unsolved problems, many of which remain unsolved today. His single most distinctive contribution was in functional analysis, in which he investigated 'Hilbert spaces' (infinite dimensional spaces). His works have significance both for pure mathematics and for mathematical physics.

HIV (Human Immunodeficiency Virus) (1983)

Robert Gallo (1937-) and Luc Montagnier (1932-)

In the 1970s it was noted that multi-partnered gay men were most likely to develop AIDS, but intravenous drug users of both sexes were also often affected. In 1982 a virus was suspected, after some haemophiliacs succumbed. This is because filtering blood serum removes bacteria and fungi, but not viruses. One theory proposed that AIDS was explained by a mutation of the swine fever virus, which at the time was decimating the pig population of Haiti. There were four groups of Haitians who seemed to be particularly at risk – homosexuals, heroin addicts, hookers and haemophiliacs.

The search for a virus in AIDS patients intensified, leading to two independent groups finding HIV at the same time. One group was at Maryland, USA, and led by Gallo, while the other was at the Pasteur Institute, Paris, led by Montagnier. Controversy as to which group was first has led Gallo, a biochemist, and Montagnier, a virologist, being honoured as joint discoverers. Although it rapidly became clear how someone catches the virus, a cure for AIDS has proved very elusive, partly because an HIV positive individual may not develop AIDS for several years, and also because the virus can rapidly change its form.

See: AIDS.

Homeostasis (1840)

Claude Bernard (1813-1878)

Among many contributions to physiology, Bernard's principal achievement was the concept of '*milieu interieur*' or homeostasis. In mammals, an unchanging internal environment is maintained through changes in the liquids bathing the cells – blood, tissue fluid and lymph. Bernard' work also showed that sugar is stored in muscles as glycogen or 'animal starch'.

Bernard's interests moved from pharmacy to playwriting to medical research. In Paris he became a student of the physiologist François Magendie. Both researchers believed knowledge could be gained only through direct experiment and were almost fanatical exponents of vivisection. Bernard's wife, an animal lover, left him in 1870.

Homo Erectus (1891)

Eugene Dubois (1858-1940)

Dubois, a Dutch anatomist, visited Sumatra in 1887, searching for signs of early man. Alfred Wallace, credited alongside Darwin for developing evolutionary theory, had suggested our ancestors came from South-East Asia. Four years later Dubois found a skull and femur in Java. After his death, other finds showed he had discovered a specimen of *Homo erectus*, the immediate ancestor of modern man. *H. erectus* had lived in Java around a million years ago.

The searches by Dubois were ignored in his lifetime, and no organisation would sponsor him. In Asia he was employed as a surgeon by the Dutch East India Company.

See: *Australopithecus africanus, Australopithecus boisei*.

Hydrogen (1766)

Henry Cavendish (1731-1810)

Cavendish, an Englishman from a rich and noble family, discovered hydrogen in 1766, as the gas liberated when iron reacted with acids. He was born in Nice, France, while his mother was making a Riviera trip for her health (although she died two years later). Cavendish spent four years at Cambridge but did not take his degree. All his life he shied away from people, and feared women intensely. For years he lived as a recluse at Clapham, London. It is said that servants had to keep out of his sight or they were sacked, and he touched little of his wealth. This included an inheritance at forty of over a million pounds, a vast fortune in those times.

In the 1770s he experimented with electricity, measuring the strength of a current by the pain of the shock it gave. He showed that hydrogen burns to form steam, and was the first to calculate the Earth's mass.

See: Deuterium, Ohm's Law.

Hypnosis (1779)

Franz Anton Mesmer (1734-1815)

Mesmer was a German graduate of the Vienna Medical School and friendly with Mozart. In Paris he set up a 'magnetic institute', in which he claimed that he could transmit 'animal magnetism', a healing force, using his hands. Some patients fell into hypnotic trances, and felt better afterwards. In 1784 a committee which included Lavoisier, Benjamin Franklin and Dr Guillotin (promoter of the guillotine) denounced him as a fake. In reality, Mesmer was a pioneer of psychiatry. His treatment by 'mesmerism' was revived in the 1840s as 'hypnotism' by J. Braid, an English surgeon. In the 1880s Freud saw at close quarters the use of hypnosis in treating emotional disorders by Josef Breuer (1842-1925) in Vienna, and then by Jean Martin Charcot (1825-1893) in Paris. In 1893 the British Medical Association accepted hypnotism as an acceptable therapeutic technique.

See: Psychoanalysis.

Icarus (1948)
Walter Baade (1893-1960)

Icarus is an unusual planetoid (asteroid) approaching within 6.5 million km (4 million miles) of the Earth. It has an elongated comet-like orbit and at one stage comes within 27 million km (17 million miles) of the Sun. Because of this it is named after the Greek mythical character who approached the Sun on wings fixed in place with wax. Icarus is one of several 'Earth-grazing' planetoids. It is unusual in coming closer to the Sun than most of the comets, and in having a large diameter, just under 1 km. Baade, a German-American astronomer, discovered it in 1948, and found it takes about 1.1 years to orbit the Sun. He made other useful findings, notably in detailed studies of the Andromeda galaxy in 1942. His studies of variable Andromedan stars known as Cepheids helped in attempts to estimate the age of the universe.

See: Big Bang.

Imprinting (1937)
Konrad Lorenz (1903-1989)

Konrad Lorenz was a distinguished Austrian animal psychologist who founded the study of animal behaviour in natural environments. His main discovery was the 'imprinting' of a newly-hatched bird – it follows the first moving thing it sees, even if it is a human, and regards it as its mother. Lorenz showed that most bird behaviour is inherited, not learned. He fought for Germany in the Second World War, ending up as a Russian prisoner of war. In 1973 he was awarded a Nobel Prize.

India from China (630)
Hsüan-Tsang (600-664)

Hs an-Tsang was a Chinese monk who was a kind of holy porter between China and India for over sixteen years. He was often referred to as 'Tripitaka', which can be translated as 'three bags full'. A convert to Buddhism, in 629 he set out for India, in spite of a ban by the Emperor on travel out of the country. He went to Bactria (Afghanistan) and then spent two years studying in Kashmir.

After visits to Madras and the Hindu Kush, he went home via the southern border of the Taklamakan Desert. After sixteen years' travelling, he translated the sacred books of Buddhism from Sanskrit into Chinese. The texts were said to be eighty-four times longer than the Bible.

India from Portugal (1498)
Vasco da Gama (1469-1525)

Vasco da Gama was the third son of a nobleman, born in Sines, south-west Portugal. In 1497 he sailed with four ships to find India. The expedition was ravaged by scurvy until they were able to procure fresh produce in Mozambique. From Kenya they crossed the Indian Ocean. In May 1498 they came to Calicut, a very important trading post of southern India. After three months' stay da Gama left, taking five Hindu hostages with him. He visited Goa and sailed back. Again, scurvy was a problem. Half the men died after the two-year voyage.

Four years later, da Gama again sailed for India, now commanding twenty vessels. From Goa he went to Cannanore (north of Calicut). Here an Arab ship was looted and set on fire, with passengers and crew locked up in the hold. The fire was kept going for four days and nights. The barbarism continued at Calicut; the town was bombarded, and thirty Hindu fishermen who had come to the ships to sell their fish were massacred. Da Gama sailed on to Cochin, and went home - hated and feared - in 1503. In 1524 he was made Governor of Portuguese India, but soon became ill with tormenting boils. He died the same year in Cochin.

See: Cape of Good Hope from Portugal.

Insects as Vectors of Disease (1895)

Sir Ronald Ross (1S57-1932)

Malaria was shown in 1880 to be caused by plasmodium, a parasitic single-celled organism. But how was the disease spread? In 1893 Patrick Manson, a physician who had worked in Hong Kong, pointed out that malaria occurs mainly in tropical swampy areas where there are plenty of mosquitoes. An English doctor, Ross, working in India, found that plasmodium spends part of its life cycle in mosquitoes of the genus Anopheles. Female anopheline mosquitoes feed on mammalian blood and, once infected with plasmodium, they can pass on the parasite to any person subsequently bitten. Ross had discovered the transmission of a disease by insect carriers or 'vectors'. Incidentally, male anopheline mosquitoes feed on plant juices and are not vectors of malaria. The ravages of malaria have been lessened considerably by killing off mosquitoes, eg by getting rid of stagnant water in which they breed.

Ross's pioneering work led Walter Reed, an American, to suspect that mosquitoes were vectors of yellow fever. In 1899 he went to Cuba to investigate an outbreak, and found the disease is carried by *Aedes aegypti* mosquitoes. Yellow fever is caused by a virus, as is typhus fever. Charles Nicolle, a bacteriologist working in Tunis, proved in 1900 that typhus is carried by body lice. Another tropical disease, African sleeping sickness (trypanosomiasis), is caused by a protozoan carried by tsetse flies. In all parts of the world, the common housefly can be a vector of a variety of diseases, from dysentery to conjunctivitis. Vectors are not of course always insects, eg bilharzia (schistosoma) is caused by a parasitic flatworm carried by water snails.

Ross first saw Britain when he was eight, having been born at Almora, India. As a young man, his main interest was in writing poetry. Encouraged by his parents, he graduated as a doctor in 1879 and joined the Indian Medical Service two years later.

See: Plasmodium Causes Malaria.

Insulin (1921)

Sir Frederick Grant Banting (1891-1941) and Charles Herbert Best (1899-1978)

In the nineteenth century, German researchers found that removing a dog's pancreas led to diabetes. In 1916 Albert Sharpey–Schafer in

Scotland suggested an antidiabetic hormone 'insulin' ('island') comes from the islets of Langerhans. These are groups of pancreatic cells, found in 1869 by a German, Paul Langerhans. Attempts to isolate insulin at first failed until, in 1921, Banting and Best tied off the duct of a dog's pancreas. This ended the production of protein-splitting enzymes in the gland, so that insulin, a protein, could be extracted. An extract from the dog's intact islets of Langerhans caused almost immediate recovery when Banting injected it into a dog dying of diabetes. Supplies of insulin for further experiments were obtained from cattle pancreases. In 1922, after trying out insulin on themselves, they injected it into fourteen-year-old Leonard Thompson, who was dying of diabetes. The boy recovered rapidly, and the path to containing the disease lay ahead. It was found the insulin extracts needed further purification to prevent toxic reactions; a method for doing this was found in 1923 by James Collip, a biochemist.

In 1921 Banting abandoned a failing orthopaedic practice in London and went to Toronto. He did not enjoy the fame that resulted from his discovery, and soon involved himself in wide-ranging research, into areas which included silicosis and aviation medicine. He was killed in a flying accident.

Best was an assistant to Professor John Macleod at Toronto University. In the summer of 1921 Macleod went for a three-month holiday in Scotland, loaning his laboratory to the two researchers. In 1923 the Nobel Prize for Physiology or Medicine was awarded to Banting and Macleod. The Nobel committee said it had not received nominations for Best or Collip, who had both contributed to producing insulin treatment. To try to compensate for the terrible decision, Banting shared his award with Best and

Macleod with Collip. Best went on to head the physiology department at Toronto (1926-1965) After Banting was killed, he also took charge of the university's Banting-Best Department for Medical Research (1941-1967).

See: Sequence of Amino Acids in Proteins and of Nucleotides in DNA.

Interference (1801)
Thomas Young (1773-1829)

In 1801 Young, an English physician, projected a narrow light beam on to a screen through two closely-spaced holes. The screen showed bands of light separated by dark bands. This cannot be explained by a particle theory of light, but is easily explained by a wave theory. A bright band occurs where two sets of waves reinforce each other. A dark band occurs where waves interfere with each other, leaving zero light energy. In 1818, Augustin Fresnel in France showed that if an interfering object is small enough, a light wave travels around it, producing a diffraction pattern.

Young was born in Milverton, Somerset, and was not long in showing his worth; he could read at the age of two. While growing up he learned to speak twelve languages and to play several musical instruments. He studied medicine at Edinburgh, and graduated from Göttingen in 1796. His talents did not lie in working with patients, but in research. He discovered the eye's property of 'accommodation' (in which the lens bulges to focus on near objects), that colour vision requires only three basic colour receptors (red, blue and green), and that light waves are transverse (rather than longitudinal), and need involve only three basic colours (red, blue and green). Not only this, he made useful contributions in other branches of physics, though the sole commemoration of these is a characteristic called Young's modulus of elasticity. He was the first person to make progress in deciphering hieroglyphics. In 1802 he became Foreign Secretary of the Royal Society, and he had a fatal heart attack in London when only fifty-six.

See: Decoding Hieroglyphics, Wave Theory of Light.

Ions are Charged Atoms (1884) and the Greenhouse Effect (1896)

Svante August Arrhenius (1859-1927)

To explain the behaviour of liquids that conduct electricity, Arrhenius, a Swede, suggested that atoms can form positively or negatively charged particles called 'ions' ('travellers'). This idea he presented in his doctoral thesis. It was then revolutionary, and he only scraped through his degree in 1884. Nineteen years later he won the Nobel Prize for Chemistry for the very same idea about ions. Arrhenius was the first to put forward what is now called the 'greenhouse effect'. He suggested that carbon dioxide could lead to global warming by letting high-frequency sunlight pass through whilst being opaque to low-frequency infra-red rays radiated from the earth at night. The action is similar to the trapping of warmth in a greenhouse. Today we know the air contains other 'greenhouse gases' (eg water vapour), and that the effect, if not controlled, will in due course lead to massive melting of the polar ice caps.

Arrhenius, born at Wijk near Uppsala, was an infant prodigy who taught himself to read when he was three. In 1895 he became a professor in Stockholm and in 1905 he was made director of the Nobel Institute for Physical Chemistry. Through studying the rates of reactions he pioneered the concept of activation energy (1889). Rather less successful was his idea that life came to Earth as spores from elsewhere in the cosmos – panspermia – which has been taken seriously by many scientists in recent decades.

Isostasy (1883)
Clarence Edward Dutton (1841-1912)

Clarence Edward Dutton was an American geologist who developed and named the concept of isostasy. This refers to the tendency of the Earth's crust to keep in a state close to equilibrium. If, for instance, the height of a mountain is reduced through erosion, compensation occurs in the form of renewed uplift. Dutton's views originated in explaining the idea of raised accumulation of sediments in mountain building. This had come from a colleague, James Hall.

Isotopes (1913)
Frederick Soddy (1877-1956)

Dalton believed that all atoms of any one element are identical. In 1913, Soddy, an Englishman, realised that an element has varieties or isotopes ('same positions'). He came to this realisation through studying radioactive decay. For instance, the decay of radium gave one product, radium D, which was found to be chemically the same as lead, so it was seen as an isotope of lead. Following the discovery of the neutron (1932), chemists realised that isotopes are structurally identical except for the number of neutrons in the nucleus. To form radium D, radium – atomic number 88 (eighty-eight protons in the nucleus) – emits three –particles. One –particle is the nucleus of a helium atom, ie two protons and two neutrons, so a radium atom losing three –particles loses six protons to form an isotope of lead (atomic number 32).

Radioactive atoms, as they give off particles, are transformed into other atoms, themselves radioactive, until a stable end product – lead – is formed. Stable atoms often possess several isotopes, differing only in the number of neutrons and in relative atomic masses.

Soddy was an assistant to Lord Rutherford. Together they studied radioactive transformations, and by 1903 they had deduced the law of radioactive decay. The term 'half-life', the time a radioactive element takes to lose half its radioactivity, was introduced at this time. Soddy concentrated on 'radio-elements' such as the so-called radium D, but did propose that tuberculosis could he treated by breathing radon, a radioactive gas (element 86) formed in the decay of radium. He was wrong, but radium therapy has proved a useful technique, eg against carcinomas.

See: α and β-Rays, Deuterium, Neutron, Proton, Radioactivity, Radium and Polonium.

Jumping Genes (1948)
Barbara McClintock (1902-1992)

Barbara McClintock suggested in 1948 that chromosomes could be unstable and that over generations, genetic material could change unpredictably. This was her main discovery during many years of research at a Long Island laboratory. Her work was largely ignored for twenty years, when she received awards, including a Nobel Prize. In 1956 she became a professor at Cornell University. Thirty-seven years before, she had gone there to read botany. Her parents showed little enthusiasm, feeling that the study of science was not feminine.

Jupiter's Satellites (1610) and Law of Falling Bodies (1604)
Galileo Galilei (1564-1642)

Galileo's report *The Sidereal Messenger* appeared in 1610 and produced much excitement. Such public interest in a scientific discovery was not seen again until Roentgen's discovery of X-rays (1895). It had all begun in 1609 when Galileo heard of a new instrument - the telescope. The enthusiasm centred on his reports of new stars and the discovery that Jupiter has four moons. Until then the accepted view was that all heavenly bodies circle the earth. The only satellite had been thought to be our Moon. With this itself Galileo created interest, with his report of mountains and 'seas' (actually dry plains) on its surface.

Galileo was born at Pisa, two months before Shakespeare. His father, a musician, was from Florence, and the family lived in that city from 1574. In 1581 Galileo returned to Pisa to study medicine. He left after four years without a degree, and in Florence he became attracted to mathematics.

In 1589 he took up a junior post at his old university, and contradicted Aristotle's view that heavy objects fall faster than light ones. The story that he demonstrated his point by dropping various objects from the Leaning Tower of Pisa is probably apocryphal.

In 1592 he became a mathematics lecturer at the University of Pisa, then one of the best in the world. He fell in love with a woman named Marina, who bore him three children. In 1610 he left Padua and Marina, but later the children joined him when she got married. His research started with advances in understanding motion. He defined acceleration, and checked his conclusion on its relation to time by experiments with a ball rolling down slopes. Observing the pendulum-like swinging of a chandelier in Pisa Cathedral, he realised that the time of one swing of a pendulum depends only on its length.

In 1609 his profitable studies of movement were set aside when he heard about the telescope. With this he could get support for the 1543 concept of Nicolaus Copernicus (1473-1543) that the sun was at the centre of the universe, with the planets circling round it. Copernicus, a Polish clergyman, feared ridicule, and his book came out only at the end of his life. His views were ignored for many years, except by Galileo and a few others. Galileo's observations confirmed the Copernican view, especially in finding Jupiter's four main satellites and in showing that Venus must circle the sun, as it displays regular phases resembling those of the Moon.

Soon Galileo became 'philosopher and chief mathematician' to the grand Duke of Tuscany, but his support of Copernican ideas disturbed the Roman Catholic Church, and he was told, on a visit to Rome, to stop. In 1632 he published a book arguing vigorously in favour of a Sun-centred system. The next year he had to return to Rome and publicly recant his theory that 'the Sun is in the centre... and the Earth is not'. Not only that, he was condemned to stay in his country house outside Florence until he died, and at first the Pope would not let him visit Florence for medical treatment.

In 1634 he became disconsolate at the death of a daughter, Veronica, at thirty-three, yet still he kept working, although he went blind in 1637. His final studies covered a variety of topics including acoustics, the motion of projectiles and the use of pendulums for time-keeping. With his achievements in mathematics, physics and astronomy, he had founded the scientific revolution.

See: Gravitation, Laws of Motion and Dispersion of White Light, Rotation of the Earth.

Krebs Cycle (1937)
Sir Hans Adolf Krebs (1900-1981)

Krebs, a distinguished biochemist, is most remembered for elucidating the stages of the Krebs or tricarboxylic acid cycle. This is a complex series of reactions by which foodstuffs are broken down with the release of usable energy. In one cycle, 18 molecules of ATP are produced. Some poisons, eg cyanides, disrupt the cycle and can cause rapid death.

Krebs was born and educated in Germany, beginning with a degree in medicine. He emigrated to England, and much of his research into chemical metabolism was done at the University of Sheffield.

See: ATP and Respiration.

L

Lake Tanganyika from England (1858)
Richard Burton (1821-1890) and
John Hanning Speke (1827-1864)

Burton was a highly talented and colourful character. In 1853, disguised as an Afghan Muslim, he journeyed to Mecca, and the next year he visited Harer, East Africa, another city forbidden to non–Muslims. He was the first European to enter Harer and come out alive. In 1855 he began an expedition with John Speke and others to try to find the source of the Nile. He was injured when their camp was attacked, and they returned home. In 1858 Burton and Speke followed up a rumour of an inland sea in East Africa. Near Ujiji, they discovered Lake Tanganyika.

Burton was very ill with malaria soon after this. Subsequently he continued his travels in Africa and Arabia, but he did not make any further discoveries. The last few years were spent in Trieste, where he continued to write prolifically. After his death, Isabel, his wife, burned all his working papers, She was deeply shocked by Burton's accounts of anthropology and Eastern erotica. He had written on pornography, homosexuality and other topics which were then taboo. An interest in such matters had begun in 1845 when the army sent him, in disguise, to investigate Karachi brothels patronised by British soldiers.

Lake Victoria from England (1858)

John Hanning Speke (1827-1864)

Speke was the discoverer – with Richard Burton – of Lake Tanganyika (1858). Following this, Speke left Burton at Tabora, and trekking due north discovered Lake Victoria. The vast size of this lake suggested that it was the Nile's source. His claim was bitterly disputed by Burton, although it was strengthened by a second expedition (1860). Speke died without learning that his theory was correct. In 1864 he shot himself accidentally while on a partridge shoot. It was not until 1875 that his view as to the Nile's source was confirmed by Henry Stanley.

See: Lake Tanganyika from England, Mountains of the Moon from USA.

Lascaux Cave Paintings (1940)

Georges Agnel (b. 1924), Simon Coencas (b. 1925), Jacques Marsal (b. 1925) and Marcel Ravidat (b. 1922)

In January 1940 these four youths from Montignac, a small town in the Vézère valley in south-west France, decided to explore a hole left by an uprooted tree and discovered by the oldest, eighteen-year-old Marcel Ravidat. Some accounts say the boys had lost a dog down the hole, but this idea is thought to have been invented by a journalist.

Once underground, the four youngsters stumbled upon a series of caverns containing an extraordinary display of prehistoric art, still the most spectacular ever found. The walls bear 17,000-year-old paintings of many kinds of animals and hunting scenes, more than 2000 figures in all. The cave's vivid depictions were recognised as prehistoric even by the young finders. As Ravidat put it in a letter to a Monsieur Laval, one of their teachers, 'a bunch of wild Indians doing a war dance wouldn't have equalled us'. It is said that Laval read the letter sceptically, but was entranced when he saw the artwork two days later. Many years earlier, the oldest palaeolithic art ever found (dated to around 26,000 BC) had been discovered, also in France, near Les Eyzies, Périgord-Quercy.

Since the discovery and exposure of the caves, human interference has led, directly or indirectly, to the deterioration of the images through exposure to damp, mould and microbial growth. Today the caves are closed to all visitors and are carefully protected.

Laws of Heredity (1864)
Gregor Johann Mendel (1822-1884)

Abbé Mendel was an amateur botanist in Brno, at that time in Austria. Between 1856 and 1863 he planted thirty-four types of peas, and then crossed twelve of them to see how characteristics appeared in succeeding generations. His brilliance lay in concentrating on one feature at a time, eg the colour of seeds (yellow or green) or their appearance (smooth or wrinkled). Statistical records of his results led him to note the laws of inheritance. These acknowledged that each characteristic was governed by factors, called genes. Mendel saw that characteristics can be 'dominant' or 'recessive', eg for pea seeds, yellow is dominant over green, making the seed with both genes yellow, and if a plant forming yellow seeds is crossed with one forming green, all the following generation will produce yellow seeds. His experiments were repeated with beans and by 1864, he could explain how characteristics are passed on from generation to generation. He wrote to Von Nägeli, a renowned Swiss botanist, who reacted negatively. Mendel returned to his monastery duties, and grew so fat he could not bend over. In 1866 a description of his findings was published in an Austrian journal, but it was ignored until 1900. Then three researchers, an Austrian, a Dutchman and a German, independently came to the same conclusions as Mendel. They were astonished to come across Mendel's paper. All three honoured the deceased Mendel as the discoverer. Soon it became clear that chromosomes are collections of genes.

See: Cell Division, DNA and RNA, Sex Chromosomes.

Laws of Planetary Motion (1609 & 1619)

Johannes Kepler (1571-1630)

In 1601 Kepler became assistant in Prague to the Dane Tycho Brahe, the most renowned pre-telescope astronomer. Using Brahe's tables of planetary positions, he obtained the first two laws. Ten years later he put forward a third law relating the times of orbit to distances from the Sun. Copernicus had assumed with the ancient Greeks that the planets move in circles, but in his first law, Kepler stated that they move in ellipses.

Newton used his laws of motion and Kepler's laws to derive the concept of gravitational attraction. In his view, the Sun and Earth attract each other with a force 'F', given by $F = GSe/d^2$, where G = a constant, S = the Sun's mass, e = Earth's mass and d = the distance between Sun and Earth. Newton went on to say that any two objects attract one another with a force quantified by a similar relationship.

Kepler's birthplace was near W rttemberg, Germany. After catching smallpox at the age of three, he was later sent to T bingen to receive a religious education. However, by 1594 he was teaching science at Graz, Austria. He then distinguished himself as a mathematician at Linz. He had to flee from Austria when the Archduke Ferdinand issued an edict condemning Protestant teachers. In 1611 Kepler lost both his wife and a child.

See: Gravitation, Laws of Motion and Dispersion of White Light

Lhasa from Goa (1716)

Ippolito Desideri (1684-1733)

Desideri, a Jesuit missionary, is recorded as the first European to reach the forbidden Tibetan capital city. In 1713 he left Goa for Delhi, and the next year made the tortuous Journey to Lhasa. He actually lived there until 1721, but had no success in setting up a Christian mission. Lamaism, the dominant Tibetan form of Buddhism, was followed steadfastly. Eventually Desideri gave up, and by 1725 had returned to his base in Portugal.

Light has a Finite Speed (1676)

Ole Christensen Romer (1644-1710)

A Danish astronomer, Romer found that the times at which Jupiter's moons seemed to pass behind the planet were not evenly spaced. The further the Earth was from Jupiter, the later eclipses of the moons seemed to occur. He decided that this was because light from the moons took longer to get to Earth when the distance was greater. From his measurements, he suggested that the speed of light was 225,000 km/sec (140,000 miles/sec). Since then, sophisticated experiments have established the value as 299,793 km/sec (186,282 miles/sec).

Romer was born at Aarhus, Jutland, and studied at Copenhagen. His pioneering observations of Jupiter's satellites were carried out in Paris. In 1681 he was called to Copenhagen to be Astronomer Royal and Professor of Astronomy.

See: Relativity Theories

LSD as a Hallucinogen (1943)

Albert Hoffman (1905-1984)

Lysergic acid occurs in ergot, but is not harmful. Poisoning by ergot is due to the formation of poisonous alkaloids. In 1943, a Swiss, Dr Hoffman, was working at the Sandoz Laboratories in Basle, looking for cures for the common cold and migraine headaches. In one experiment he succeeded in attaching a diethylamide group to lysergic acid, obtaining lysergic acid diethylamide tartrate – LSD. Its mind-bending properties quickly affected Hoffman, as only a tiny quantity of the compound is effective. In the early 1940s there were several studies of its hallucinogenic and dream-inducing properties, but researchers also looked into its medical possibilities. It was employed from 1961 by the Dutchman Jan Bastiaans, and other psychiatrists, as a way to open up distressing recollections which had been repressed.

In 1966 the Sandoz Corporation stopped all production of 'acid', disturbed by its increasing use as a psychedelic drug. It is still available however, being made in at least five countries.

See: Acetylcholine

Magnetism (550 BC)
Thales of Miletus (c.620 c.555 BC)

Magnetism was discovered as a property of lodestone (magnetic oxide of iron, FE_3O_4). In Europe this was first found in the administrative region of Magnisia in central Greece, giving rise to the name 'magnet'. The first record of magnetism was by Thales at Miletus. The exact place and date of the discovery are not known. Using a magnetised needle as a compass was a later discovery. It has been said that in ancient times, a camel tram could cross the Gobi desert because the leading animal carried a hanging lump of lodestone or 'leading stone'. Possibly the Chinese gave the idea to the Arabs, who then passed it on to Europeans. Compasses started to be used in Europe during the twelfth century.

See: Earth is a Magnet

Mecca from Italy (1503)
Ludovico Di Varthema (c. 1475-1530)

Ludovico Di Varthema is the first Christian and European recorded as having safely visited the holy Islamic city. In 1502 he left Venice for six years of travel and adventure. At Damascus, dressed as a Muslim pilgrim, he joined a caravan going to Mecca. Leaving undetected, he travelled to many places in Asia. In Aden, arrested as a Christian spy, he was freed by the Sultan after pretending to be mad.

Mecca, in Saudi Arabia, was the birthplace of Muhammad, Islam's founder. Pilgrimage to the city (Hajj) is one of the Five Pillars of Islam. Muslims must turn towards the city five times each day to pray. Di Varthema would have been killed in Mecca if his true identity had become known.

See: Lake Tanganyika from England

Micro-Organisms (1676)

Antonie van Leeuwenhoek (1632-1723)

This Dutchman was the first to make a small magnifying glass powerful enough to act as a simple microscope. He succeeded in grinding tiny, accurately-curved lenses that could magnify up to two hundred times. In long letters to the Royal Society in London, he described his findings. These included 'animalcules' (protista) in stagnant water – living organisms which are too small to be seen by the eye alone. Soon after this discovery, he came across 'germs' (bacteria). He also saw for the first time yeast cells, red blood cells and blood flowing through a tadpole's rail. An assistant, Johann Ham, discovered sperm cells.

Van Leeuwenhoek was a merchant in Delft, the Netherlands, until he became famous as a microscopist. The Royal Society elected him a fellow, and visitors included the Queen of England and the Russian Tsar.

Minoan Civilisation (1894)

Sir Arthur John Evans (1851-1941)

Evans, a British archaeologist, was inspired by Schliemann's successes in locating ancient Greek cities. A dig on the island of Crete eventually unearthed a highly-organised, lavishly-decorative civilisation stretching back many centuries before the time of Homer. In Greek legend, a powerful early civilisation was built up in Crete under King Minos. It ended mysteriously and suddenly in about 1450 BC.

See: Mycenae.

Mount Kilimanjaro from Germany (1848)

Johannes Rebmann (1820-1876)

Johannes Rebmann was a German missionary and explorer. He and his associate, Johann Krapf (1810-1881), were the first to venture inland from what is now Mombasa. Rebmann was the first European to sight Africa's highest mountain, Mount Kilimanjaro (5,895m or 19,340 ft). The following year Krapf was the first European to see Mount Kenya.

Mountains of the Moon from the USA (1889)

Henry Morton Stanley (1841-1904)

Stanley was born in Wales and went to the USA in 1859. In 1869 came his famous assignment for the *New York Herald*, to find what had happened to Livingstone. His adventure gave him a desire to explore, and he returned to East Africa in 1874. In 1875 he found that Speke's conviction that Lake Victoria was the source of the Nile was right. Subsequently, in three expeditions, Stanley sailed along the Lualaba and Congo rivers. At the end of the first expedition, in 1877, only one hundred and fourteen of three hundred and fifty-six followers were still alive. The third expedition (1888) involved incredible hardship, including many murders of porters by pygmies. Stanley was said to have led with the ruthlessness of a slave trader. Of the original group of seven hundred followers, half never reached home.

Towards the end of this grim journey, Stanley discovered the Semliki river and the Mountains of the Moon (the Ruwenzori Range). *See: Central and East Africa from South Africa, Lake Victoria from England.*

Mycenae (1876)

Heinrich Schliemann (1822-1890)

As a boy, Schliemann was fascinated by Homer and dreamed of finding the city of Troy. Following astonishing successes in Asia Minor, he moved to mainland Greece and organised a dig at the site of Mycenae. According to Homer, this had once been the great city of Agamemnon, who had led the Greek side in the Trojan War. The digging led to the discovery of a ruined city, with massive outer walls, built around 1500 BC. Schliemann had become obsessed with the Trojan War. He worked himself up from grocery assistant to wealthy businessman. Then at the age of forty-six he left Germany for Turkey to begin archaeological explorations.

Natural Opiates (1974)
John Hughes (1940-) and Hans Kosterlitz (1938-1996)

At the University of Aberdeen, Scotland, Professor Kosterlitz and Dr Hughes investigated extracts from the brains of over 2000 pigs. They isolated two compounds with similar actions to morphine – relieving pain and inducing pleasure. The substances were named encephalins, meaning 'in the head'. Later, other naturally-occurring compounds, with larger molecules, were discovered. These are the endorphins (endogenous morphines). Encephalitis and endorphins have molecules that are chemically different from morphine, but architecturally similar. The endorphins are messenger molecules in the brain. They are responsible for the runner's high and the delay in feeling pain after a violent injury. One researcher writes that they induce euphoria in investigators as well as in experimental animals!

Natural Selection (1845)
Charles Robert Darwin (1809-1882)

The mechanism of evolution was discovered by Darwin, who destroyed the view that mankind is a unique creation. His concept was that, for any form of life, when a particular variation allowed it to survive more easily in an environment, the variation could be perpetuated, producing divergence from the original form. In this way, species of all living things develop from earlier forms.

Shrewsbury-born Darwin was a physician's son. In 1825 he began studying medicine at Edinburgh, transferring, in 1827, to Cambridge with the aim of becoming a clergyman. Participating in talks and field trips led by the professors of botany and geology focused his interest in the natural world. After graduating in 1831 he sailed as a naturalist on HMS *Beagle*, which made a five-year survey of the South American coasts. Darwin made a host of useful observations in biology, anthropology and geology. By 1846, reports on the *Beagle* studies had been completed and he began to write out his views on evolution.

In 1858 he was astounded to get a letter from Malaysia written by another Englishman, Alfred Wallace (1823-1913). The missive summarised Darwin's ideas. Wallace, however, came to favour a supernatural explanation of man's intelligence and awareness.

The Origin of Species by Means of Natural Selection (1859) was the first of a series of erudite books which explained evolution, and foresaw most scientific objections to his theory. In 1833 Darwin married his cousin, Emma Wedgwood. They moved in 1842 to Down House (at Downe, Kent), where Darwin was a semi-invalid for many years. He had four sons. At the age of seventy-three he died at Downe from a heart attack.

See: Plutonic Theory of Earth's Origin.

Neptune (1846)

Urbain le Verrier (1811-1877)

Neptune was the last of the eight true planets to be discovered, Pluto (discovered in 1930 by Clyde Tombaugh) having recently been demoted to dwarf planet status. It was the great Italian scientist Galileo who appears to have first observed Neptune, having recorded it through his telescope on a star map in 1613, but he counted it as an ordinary star, as it was at a point in its orbit where its apparent motion is barely noticeable.

In the 19th century, observations of Uranus, then the outermost known planet, suggested that an undiscovered body was perturbing its orbit, and John Couch Adams in England and Urbain Le Verrier in France began to try to calculate its movements. On September 23 1846, Johann Gottfried Galle and Heinrich d'Arrest at the Berlin Observatory received a letter from Le Verrier giving them a position. That same night they found the planet within one degree of Le Verrier's predicted location. We now know that Neptune is almost as large as Uranus and slightly more massive, and orbits a billion miles further out. Initially John Couch Adams was given equal credit for the discovery, but as Le Verrier's position was much more accurate and it was his letter which prompted the successful search, he has now been declared the official discoverer.

Le Verrier was born in Saint-Lô, Manche, and studied chemistry before going into astronomy, spending most of his career at the Paris Observatory, where in 1854 he became Director. His name is one of the 72 names of great French scientists and engineers inscribed on the Eiffel Tower. He was much less successful as a manager than as a scientist, and was at one stage forced to stand down from his directorship after clashes with the observatory staff. He died in Paris, leaving a wife and children.

Neutron (1932)

Sir James Chadwick (1891-1974)

In 1930 W. Bothe and H. Becker in Germany bombarded the element beryllium with -rays and found that a mysterious, highly-penetrative radiation was released from the nucleus. Two years later, F. and I. Joliot-Curie in France found that the rays from beryllium would knock protons out of paraffin wax, a compound of hydrogen and carbon. Chadwick, a British physicist, was quick to see that the new radiation was streams of particles. Experiments showed him that the particles – 'neutrons' – were uncharged and had masses almost identical to protons. It was soon apparent that an atomic nucleus cotains neutrons and protons packed together. The sole exception is hydrogen-1, in which the nucleus consists of a single proton. Because neutrons are electrically neutral, they can easily penetrate the nucleus and have proved invaluable in atomic research.

Chadwick graduated from Manchester University in 1911, and then worked in Berlin. He was interned during the First World War. Subsequently, he held various positions in Cambridge, where he discovered the neutron, and in Liverpool, where he helped to build the first British cyclotron (particle accelerator).

See: α *and* β *Rays, Deuterium, Isotopes, Proton.*

Niger River from Morocco (1351)

Sheik Muhammed Ibn-Abdullah Ibn
Battutah (1304-1368)

Ibn Battutah was an insatiable traveller from Tangier. Over a 30-year period he travelled in Africa, Asia and Asia Minor, visiting nearly every Muslim country. Although he discovered new territory, he was the first true explorer of Arabia. In one of several long-distance expeditions, he went to northern Africa from 1349-1353. In that time, he came across the Niger river near Djenné, and visited Timbuktu, Kabare and Tamanrasset. Ibn Battutah obtained two wives on the way to Mecca, and a further three in the Maldive Islands. *See: Timbuktu from England.*

Nitrocellulose (1845)

Christian Frederick Schönbein (1799-1868)

The explosives industry had its foundation in an accidental discovery by this German chemist. While working in the kitchen, he spilt a mixture of nitric acid and sulphuric acid on to a cotton apron. The apron, after being hung up to dry, exploded. Nitrocellulose - much more powerful than gunpowder - had been discovered. Schönbein was none too popular with his wife, who considered it out of order for experiments to be done in her kitchen! Schönbein was born in Metzingen and educated at T bingen and Erlangen. He joined Basel University in 1828 and became a professor there seven years later. In 1839, investigating a strange odour often smelt near electrical apparatus, he discovered ozone, a form of oxygen. He passed away at Sauersberg, Baden, remaining to the end a non-believer in the atomic theory.

See: Ozone Layer.

Nuclear Fission (1939)

Otto Robert Frisch (1904-1979), Otto Hahn (1879-1968) and Lise Meitner (1878-1968)

In 1912 Lise Meitner, an Austrian, joined Hahn at the Kaiser Wilhelm Institute in Berlin. As a female, she was forbidden to enter the main building! Their great joint successes were in the 1930s, investigating the products of bombarding uranium with neutrons. Being Jewish, Lise Meitner had to flee from the Nazis to Stockholm in 1938. The next year she wrote a letter to the British journal *Nature*, explaining Hahn's finding that the neutron bombardment was producing an element half the mass of uranium - barium. Her idea was that fission had occurred, splitting the uranium nucleus in two.

Meitner worked with her nephew, Otto Frisch, on the theory of nuclear fission, which led to producing nuclear chain reactions and nuclear bombs. When he was young, Frisch Worked in Vienna and Berlin, but left Germany for the same reason as Meitner. He then did nuclear research in London, Copenhagen and Birmingham. Surprisingly, the German, Hahn, was awarded a Nobel Prize (1944), but Meitner and Frisch were not.

See: Artificial Radioactivity, Radioactivity.

Nuclear Magnetic Resonance (Magnetic Resonance Imaging) (1946)

Felix Bloch (1905-1983) and
Edward Mills Purcell (1912-1997)

In NMR an area to be examined is put in a high-intensity magnetic field, causing alignment of atomic nuclei. As soon as the field is cut off the atoms revert to their original states, emitting radio signals from which the patterns of the elements can he revealed. This modern method of body scanning - to 'see' what is invisible - is of great diagnostic value in medicine, together with CAT, computerised axial tomography, and utilises X-ray beams as scanners. NMR is also known as MRI – magnetic resonance imaging. This was developed in America, thirty years after a 1946 intensive study of magnetic resonance. It was found possible to locate the positions within molecules even of hydrogen atoms, the tiniest of all atoms. Two independent teams discovered the principles of NMR, one team led by Bloch, a Swiss-born US physicist, the other by Purcell, a US radiation expert. In 1951 this latter researcher was the first to detect the 'song of hydrogen' (radio waves emitted by hydrogen in outer space). It was fair that in 1952 Bloch shared the Nobel Prize for Physics with Purcell for their work in magnetic resonance.

Bloch, born in Z rich, obtained his PhD and first academic post at Leipzig. In 1933 he left Germany and the next year began researching in the States. Purcell was born in Illinois, graduated from Purdue (1933) and gained a doctorate from Harvard (1938). He has carried out significant researches in radio astronomy.

See: Electromagnetic Waves.

Oceanography (1848)
Matthew Fontaine Maury (1806-1873)

Physical Geography of the Sea, the first textbook of ocean studies, was published by Maury in 1855. He was a US naval officer who charted the Gulf Stream and other ocean currents. His enthusiasm began in his early thirties following an accident that made him lame. Put in charge of the depot for charts and instruments, he became the initiator of extensive studies of oceanic waters, especially their currents. Maury is best known for studying the Gulf Stream, first investigated in 1769 by Benjamin Franklin.

Ohm's Law (1827)
Georg Simon Ohm (1787-1854)

Ohm, a German mathematician and physicist, gained fame for studying the resistance of electrical conductors to electrical flow. He found that resistance relates precisely to the size of the current passing under a known electromotive force (or 'electrical push'). For a conductor at constant temperature, the potential difference (in volts) divided by the current (in amperes) gives the conductor's resistance (in ohms).

$$\text{In brief: ohms} = \frac{\text{volts}}{\text{amps}}$$

The best conductor has been shown to be pure silver. Ohm's law had been discovered many years earlier by Henry Cavendish, but he had not published his results. Ohm, a motor mechanic's son, became a high school teacher, but longed for a university appointment. However, after devising his law, he remained a very poor man for six years, without even a school position. Eventually renown came his way, and in 1349 – at the age of sixty – he achieved his heart's desire and became a professor at Munich University. *See: Electric Current, Hydrogen.*

Origin of Coal (1836)
William Logan (1798-1875)

Logan, a Canadian geologist, solved the problem of how coal originates. Whilst working in Wales, he investigated rocks lying below coal seams and discovered stigmaria, the pitted underground parts of fossil trees such as sigillaria. This led to the realisation that coal is derived from ancient plant material, which gives rise to peat. This becomes lignite (soft coal) and gradually increases in carbon content, becoming bituminous coal and eventually anthracite.

Later, Logan set out to map Canada by canoe. His travels led him to make major geological discoveries.

Oxygen (1771)

Carl Wilhelm Scheele (1742-1786) and
Joseph Priestley (1733-1804)

Oxygen gas was first isolated in 1771 by Scheele, a Swede. Sadly, his publisher did not release his report of the discovery of 'fire air' until six years later. Meanwhile, in 1774 Priestley, an Englishman, independently produced 'dephlogisticated air', which was the same element. So both men can be credited with discovering oxygen. Possibly they both used the same method – heating mercury oxide.

Scheele was born near Stralsund, Pomerania, then a Swedish province. He was the seventh child of eleven, and became an apothecary's apprentice when he was fourteen. His chemical knowledge, largely self-taught, inspired him to discover four acids – citric, lactic, tartaric and uric. He also investigated hydrogen fluoride, hydrogen sulphide and hydrogen cyanide, and even recorded the taste of the latter, a deadly poisonous compound. Not only did Scheele discover oxygen, he was involved in the discovery of six other elements (barium, chlorine, manganese, molybdenum, nitrogen and tungsten). Only the discovery of chlorine is credited to Scheele, who has been called 'the world's unluckiest chemist'. Most of his life was spent in chemical research. Social life was not for him, and it was only on his deathbed that he married. When he was only forty-four, he suffered a fatal collapse at Köping, Sweden.

Priestley, a Yorkshireman, was brought up by a pious aunt after his mother died when he was seven. His father was a nonconformist minister, and he became a Unitarian preacher. In 1766, after meeting Benjamin Franklin in London, he became intrigued by electricity, and later discovered that carbon is a conductor. His work in chemistry was mainly with oxygen and other gases, which he collected over mercury. Priestley, a cold, prim character, became unpopular for sympathising with American colonists in their war against George III, and later with French revolutionaries. In 1791 a mob burned down his house in Birmingham. He escaped to London and left in 1794 for America. He died at Northumberland in Pennsylvania at the age of 71.

See: *Air is a Mixture* and *Significance of Oxygen*.

Ozone Layer (1913)

Charles Fabry (1867-1945)

Ultraviolet rays in sunlight act on oxygen molecules (O-O or O_2) in air to produce molecules of ozone (O_3). This uses up radiation which would otherwise penetrate the atmosphere in concentrations dangerous to life. The concentration of ozone is highest (one volume to four million volumes of air) at a height of 24 km (15 miles). This 'ozone layer' was discovered by Fabry, a French physicist. Concern about breakdown of parts of the ozone layer commenced in the 1960s, when it was realised that CFCs (chlorofluorocarbons) in the air decompose very slowly and tend to destroy ozone (by reacting with it).

Marseilles-born Fabry obtained a doctorate in 1892 and took the Sorbonne Chair in Physics in 1920. He specialised in optics and spectra.

See: *Oxygen*.

P

Pacific Islands from England (1769-1773)
James Cook (1728-1779)

Cook was the son of a Yorkshire farm worker who had nine children altogether. As a young man he showed himself to be a skilled seaman, navigator and map-maker. In 1768 he was chosen to lead a scientific expedition to the Pacific, which began with observing a transit of Venus from Tahiti. Sailing on through the South Seas, he discovered the two islands forming New Zealand, separated by what we now call the Cook Strait. Then, striking westwards, in 1770 he came to Australia. He claimed a region he named 'New South Wales' for Britain and successfully navigated the Great Barrier Reef. Subsequently he sailed to Java, anchored at Jakarta and established that Sumatra and Java are separate.

By now, nearly everyone on board was suffering from dysentery or malaria, and thirty died. No one developed scurvy, however, thanks to Cook's insistence on a diet that included vegetables, and fresh fruit when possible.

From 1772 to 1775, he became the first to sail around the planet from west to east. During the voyage he visited Easter Island, with its strange statues, and New Caledonia. In 1776 Cook tried to discover the 'North-West Passage', a supposed northern route from the Atlantic to the Pacific. On this voyage, he discovered Christmas Island and the Hawaiian Islands. Early in 1779 an argument with Hawaiian Islanders broke out following the pilfering of tools and the stealing of a small boat. This led to fighting in which Cook was stabbed and clubbed to death. He had provided cartographers with more extensive and accurate information about the world than has ever been given before by one person.

See: Australia from Netherlands, Easter Island from Netherlands, Tasmania, New Zealand, Tonga and Fiji from Netherlands.

Penicillin (1928)

Sir Alexander Fleming (1881-1955)

Fleming worked for forty-nine years at St Mary's Hospital in London. In 1928 he went for a three-week holiday, leaving a culture dish on which pus-forming bacteria were growing. The culture became contaminated with spores of mould, probably from a laboratory beneath. By good luck the weather was cold, letting the mould grow, and then warmed up, enabling the bacteria to flourish. On returning, Fleming was astounded to find that the mould had killed all the bacteria near it.

The mould was *Penicillin notatum*, and Fleming called the substance that had seeped out from it penicillin. For eight weeks he experimented with his antibiotic, which seemed effective. He did not see its extraordinary potential, however. This was partly because it seemed to lose its power when mixed with blood in a test tube. Success was due to Howard Florey, an Australian pathologist, and Ernst Chain, a Jewish biochemist, working together in Oxford. Searching for information about antibacterial chemicals,

Chain found the report about *Penicillin notatum*. The laboratory had some of this mould. Florey and Chain soon discovered that the liquid it releases contains only one part in two million of penicillin. Showing great resourcefulness, the researchers, aided by Norman Heatley, a biochemist colleague, succeeded by 1941 in purifying and testing penicillin. In July of that year, Florey and Heatley went to the USA to get help in developing large-scale production. Mass production of penicillin started in 1943, and rapidly the drug showed its fantastic effectiveness. In 1945 Florey, Chain and Fleming received the Nobel Prize, although it was through the efforts of Florey, Chain and Heatley that penicillin reached the world.

Today there is a whole range of antibiotics. In January 1996 a slide bearing a descendant of the original mould was sold at auction for £15,000, and two months later a second such slide was sold for £20,000.

Periodic Table of Elements (1869)
Dmitri Ivanovich Mendeleyev (1834-1907)

In the nineteenth century the list of elements grew, and several chemists looked tor a pattern. In France in 1862 de Chancourtois suggested that elements should be arranged in order of increasing atomic mass. Two years later, in England, Newlands had a similar idea, and pointed out a close likeness between each element and the one eight places below and above it. Both proposals were ignored, and Newlands was ridiculed. The eight places of his scheme were mockingly compared to the eight notes of a musical octave!

It was the Russian, Mendeleyev, who showed that a table of elements according to atomic mass is periodic, ie similar elements appear at periodic intervals. Where properties put an element out of order, he boldly altered the order. Today we know that the order of the table refers to increasing atomic number (number of protons in the nucleus). This is a little different to Mendeleyev's order according to increasing atomic mass. In the periodic table, the vertical columns contain 'groups' or 'families' of elements. Group 1, for instance, is the alkali metals. We can marvel from this group alone at Mendeleyev's achievement. Francium was not discovered until 1939, and he may not have known of the discovery of caesium (1860) or rubidium (1861).

Notice that sodium is an example of the partial correctness of Newlands' view. It has atomic number 11, ie there are eleven protons in the sodium nucleus. Eight places below it is the closely similar element lithium, and eight places above it the very similar element potassium.

GROUP 1: ALKAL1 METALS

Element	Atomic No	Atomic Mass
lithium	3	7
sodium	11	23
potassium	19	39
rubidium	37	85.5
caesium	55	133
francium	87	233

Mendeleyev triumphed in leaving certain holes in his table, and in three cases predicting the properties of the missing elements. The three elements were discovered in his lifetime; gallium in 1875, scandium in 1879 and germanium in 1886. Their properties were extraordinarily close to what he had predicted. His birthplace was at Tobolsk, Siberia. He was the youngest of a very large family. When he was small, his father – a school principal – went blind, and his mother set up a glass factory. In 1849 he joined a college in St Petersburg, leaving top of the class six years later. By 1866 he was a professor of chemistry in the city, and known as a brilliant lecturer and textbook writer. In 1876 he divorced his wife and married a young art student. Being the great Mendeleyev, he was safe from censure. His views were decidedly liberal, and in 1890 he resigned from his position because of oppression of students by the authorities.

See: Alkali Metals and Alkaline-Earth Metals, Atomic Masses, Elements, Proton.

Peru from Spain (1531)

Francisco Pizarro (L. 1475-1541)

Francisco Pizarro was the Spanish conquistador who caused the collapse of the society of the Incas. His early years were a tough, peasant existence, similar to that of Cortés, who was a distant relative. When he was about fifty he sailed off with Diego de Almagro to explore South America. In 1529 he was appointed Governor of New Castillo, a province south of Panama. In 1531 he set out with one hundred and eighty men and thirty-seven horses to conquer Peru and the Incas. The party crossed the Andes and was met at Cajamarca by Atahualpa, emperor of the Incas. Pizarro's men attacked, and over nine thousand Incas were massacred. The Emperor ransomed himself for as much gold as would fill a room in the palace. Nevertheless, Pizarro had him garrotted, and went to sack Cuzco city. His prestige in Spain grew very high, but in 1541 he was killed by a man sent by Almagro, who had become very jealous of his former friend.

See: Aztec Empire from Spain.

Phagocytosis (1883)

Ilya Ilich Mechnikoff (1545-1916)

Mechnikoff, a Russian zoologist, investigated sea anemones in Sicily. He found they possess amoeba-like cells which can engulf bacteria and tiny particles. In 1888 he became Pasteur's most devoted student in Paris, and later succeeded him as Head of the Pasteur Institute. He is noted as the discoverer of phagocytosis, in which white blood cells engulf bacteria. An eccentric individual, Mechnikoff always wore overshoes, and carried an umbrella out of doors, whatever the weather. He was born in Ivanovka, Ukraine, the son of an officer of the Imperial Guard. After graduating in Kharkov, he worked in Germany and then Russia. In 1873 he tried to poison himself after the death of his wife. In 1882 he resigned to concentrate on research. His work included ways of prolonging life, but he died in Paris when he was seventy-one.

Photoelectric Effect (1902)

Philipp Eduard Anton Lenard (1862-1947)

Lenard, a German, discovered that if light strikes the surfaces of certain metals, it causes electrons to be emitted. The effect was soon utilised in the photoelectric cell, an essential component in sending information by fax (facsimile transmission). When Lenard's finding became known, physicists were intrigued to discover that changing the wavelength of the light had an effect, eg yellow light makes electrons fly out at lower speeds than blue light. This was inexplicable until Einstein showed that a simple answer lies in Planck's quantum theory. For this explanation (and not for relativity theory) Einstein was given the 1921 Nobel Prize for Physics. Lenard himself won the 1905 prize, and was a pioneer of research into cathode rays and atomic structure at Heidelberg and Kiel. In his lectures he showed great dislike for British scientists, especially Newton- he could not stand even to speak his name, to see it or hear it! Lenard's principal position was as Professor of Theoretical Physics at Heidelberg. He retired from that post in 1931, and subsequently became a fanatical supporter of Hitler and Nazism.

See: Electron, Quantum Theory.

Piezoelectricity (1880) and Curie Temperature (1895)

Pierre Curie (1859-1906)

Pierre Curie, helped by his brother Jacques, found that a voltage develops across certain crystals if pressure is applied to them. Conversely, if a voltage is applied to such crystals, they constrict as if they are being put under pressure. In 1895 Pierre married Marie, and later they were the co-discoverers of radium and polonium. That same year, Pierre discovered that at a certain temperature a magnetic substance loses its magnetism. This temperature became known as the Curie temperature. In 1896 Marie found a way of utilising piezoelectricity to measure the radiation given off by uranium. Soon her husband dropped his own work, and for the rest of his life was an eager second to her. He died in 1906 when his head was crushed by a wagon wheel.

See: Radium and Polonium, Ultrasonics.

Plasmodium Causes Malaria (1880)

Charles Louis Alphonse Laveran (1845-1922)

Not long ago, over one-tenth of the world suffered from malaria. The cause was widely thought to be bad air ('mala aria' in Italian) in swampy areas. In 1880 Laveran, a French bacteriologist, found that sufferers have in their red blood cells parasitic protozoa of the genus Plasmodium. Protozoa are single-celled animals, including the well-known amoeba. Laveran was awarded the 1907 Nobel Prize for Medicine and Physiology.

A Parisian, he qualified as a doctor at Strasbourg (1867) and became a military surgeon. His 1880 discovery, the first time a disease was seen as caused by protozoa not bacteria, was made in Algeria. After leaving the army, Laveran worked at the Pasteur Institute in Paris.

See: Insect Vectors of Disease.

Pleasure Centre (1954)

James Olds (1922-1976)

Olds, a US physiologist, discovered an astounding function of the hypothalamus, a centre within the brain containing various devices for controlling body function. He found a region that produces sensations of intense pleasure if it is stimulated. When an electrode connected to a rat's pleasure centre was set up, so the rat itself could make a tiny current flow, the animal kept producing the stimulation. It had no interest in food, sleep or sex, but would stimulate its pleasure centre about twice a second, for hours at a time. Olds and his co-workers suggested that anything desirable to a mammal has desire only to the extent that it stimulates the pleasure centre. Much, however, remains to be learned about the working of the hypothalamus.

Olds obtained a doctorate from Harvard in 1952. He researched at McGill, Los Angeles and Michigan into brain stimulation. From 1967 to 1976 he worked at the California Institute of Technology, mainly on how learning is achieved. A heart attack caused his death at the age of fifty-four.

Plutonic Theory of Earth's Origin (1795)
James Hutton (1726-1797)

The plutonic theory sees heat as the main agent of the elevation of land masses. In 1788 Hutton envisaged an unconformity – a fossil surface of erosion – as evidence of time's vast span. This supported belief in multiple cycles of uplift and erosion. Hutton's theory refers to a self-renewing 'world machine'. There is an endlessly repeated cycle of three stages: 1) breakdown (eg action of waves on rocks); 2) parts of old continents laid down in ocean basins; and 3) expansion due to heat produces new continents at sides of old oceans (and erosion of old continents produces new oceans).

Hutton was a wealthy intellectual who lived in Edinburgh at a time when David Hume, Adam Smith and James Watt also lived

there. In 1749 he obtained a medical degree at Leiden, but never practised. He was upset when called an atheist because of his view of natural change ('...we find no vestige of a beginning - no prospect of an end'). An attempt to clarify matters with a second book failed, as most of it was unreadable. His theory was made clear in 1802 in a hook written by John Playfair, a mathematics professor and a close friend of Hutton. Shortly before his death he worked on a book which anticipated Darwin's concepts of evolution.
See: Natural Selection.

Pompeii and Herculaneum (1748)

Rocco Gioacchino de Alcubierre (1712-1790)

In the year AD 79, the Roman Pliny the Younger saw Vesuvius erupt. He described how the city of Pompeii disappeared in a sea of ash, while nearby Herculaneum was covered by boiling mud. Both towns were partially dam aged by looters, then totally abandoned. A low hill covered the place where Pompeii had stood, known to locals as 'la civila' (the city).

In 1592 an Italian engineer, Domenico Fontana (1543-1607) was amazed to discover buried ruins. He was making a tunnel beneath a hill whilst setting up an aqueduct. Serious excavation did not begin until the early eighteenth century. The Austrians, then ruling Naples, had statues plundered and sent to Vienna. In 1748 the first thoroughgoing examinations at Pompeii were made by Rocco de Alcubierre, a surveying engineer. Unfortunately, he too was a treasure-seeker, sent by Charles III of Spain. Soon he transferred his attention to Herculaneum, and excavating Pompeii did not begin in earnest until 1754. The excavations were disorganised, and an antiquities expert who toured the sites in 1762 wrote, 'Alcubierre knows as much of antiquities as the moon does of lobsters". The Spanish engineer was under orders to supply his court with precious objects, but wanton damage occurred under his direction. However, the discoveries set alight the imagination of Europe. When Alcubierre was promoted to Colonel and Chief Engineer at Naples, Karl Weber was made Director of Excavations at Pompeii. This Swiss officer began systematic excavating, and recording and care of artefacts. Nevertheless, for some years the excavator's main aim was to discover statues, gold Jewellery and other treasures. It was not until 1860 that fully organised scientific exploration commenced, led by Giuseppe Fiorelli, an Italian numismatist.

Positron (1932)
Carl David Anderson (1905-1991)

The antielectron or positively-charged electron turned up two years after Dirac had predicted it could exist. In America, Anderson was working with Robert Millikan on cosmic rays, which Millikan felt could well be electromagnetic radiation (not particles). In Anderson's famous experiment, cosmic rays passed through a lead sheet knocked out particles that were identical to electrons, but were positively charged.

In 1930 Anderson obtained his doctorate from the California Institute of Technology. Five years later his experiments led to the discovery of another subatomic particle, the mu-meson. This was less dramatic than the discovery of the positron, the first particle of antimatter to be shown to exist.

See: Antimatter, Cosmic Rays, Electron.

Proton (1914)

Baron Rutherford of Nelson (Sir Ernest Rutherford)
(1871-1937)

Channel rays, discovered in 1886 by Goldstein, moved the opposite way from negatively charged cathode rays. Experiments showed that the rays contain the fundamental positive particle, which Lord Rutherford called 'proton' (from the Greek term for 'first'). The proton proved to be the unit of positive charge, just as the electron is the unit of negative charge.

Between 1906 and 1908 Rutherford was experimenting with the firing of rays at thin metal foils. Usually the rays went straight through, but some particles bounced back. He said it was like firing bullets at sheets of paper, and discovering some bullets bounce off. His deduction was that the bounced particles had struck a dense core in the atom. It was so small that most -rays passed through undeflected. Rutherford's discovery showed the incorrectness of Dalton's concept of atoms as tiny indivisible balls. Instead the bulk of the mass of an atom was seen to be concentrated in the central core or 'nucleus'. This is made of protons, a different number for each element. Around the nucleus are electrons, equal in number to the protons, but very much lighter.

See: - and -Rays, Atom, Atomic Theory, Cathode Rays and Channel Rays, Electron, Isotopes.

Psychoanalysis (1892)

Sigmund Freud (1856-1939)

Freud has perhaps had a greater effect upon the lives of modern westerners than any other scientific figure. Initially he outraged many with his views that people are not rational, that there is very little difference between abnormality and normality, and that children have sexuality (eg the Oedipus complex in boys). He was born in Freiberg, Moravian Germany (now Pribor, Czech Republic), and was christened Sigismund, which he changed in 1875 to Sigmund. His Jewish father had a second wife half his age and two adult sons from a previous marriage. The family moved to Vienna in 1860, and Freud read medicine at its university from 1873-1881. He took several years to graduate because of wide intellectual interests, which included psychology.

In 1877 his first scientific paper dealt with experiments confirming that male eels have testes. In 1882 he began working at a hospital in Vienna, ending up on the staff of T. Meynert, an expert on brain anatomy. His patients included many with 'hysteria', and he was fascinated by the use of hypnosis by a friend, Josef Breuer. In 1885 Freud studied in Paris with Jean Martin Charcot, who often used hypnosis in treating hysterical patients. His experiences there led Freud to pioneer tree association, in which patients were encouraged to talk freely. The technique worked well, often allowing repressed memories to be released. Freud said he gave patients 'a rail ticket to normality', but they had to decide if they wished to travel.

At the end of the century, Freud decided that the cause of female hysteria was real or imagined attempts at incest on young children by fathers. Early in the twentieth century he came to see the mind as having three conflicting aspects: ego, superego and id. The ego's compromises between conflicting demands normally emerge as dreams and defence mechanisms, such as sublimation.

In 1909 Freud visited America, where Freudian therapy was soon taken up by many doctors. Soon after this, rival schools were set up, the first by Alfred Adler (1870-1937) who felt man's longing for power was more significant than sexual desires. In 1914 Carl Jung (1875-1961) founded 'analytical psychology', considering Freud was making too much of childhood sexuality. The values of psychoanalysis, including understanding the unconscious mind and doctor-patient relationships, became more and more apparent.

Freud fell in love with a Martha Bernys in 1882, but could not afford to marry until four years later. They had six children. Anna, the youngest, became an influential child psychologist. In 1933 Hitler banned psychoanalysis, and in 1938, when the Nazis seized power, the family moved to London. Freud died at the age of eighty-three from cancer of the jaw, probably caused by excessive smoking of cigars.

See: Hypnosis.

Pulsars (1967)

Susan Jocelyn Bell Burnell (1943-)

Jocelyn Bell, born in Belfast, Northern Ireland, discovered objects in the sky which were emitting regular pulses of radio waves. At first she and Antony Hewish, her supervisor, wondered if aliens were trying to make contact, and the first sources found were represented as 'LGM' (Little Green Men). In fact the sources were pulsars, rotating neutron stars giving out short bursts of radio waves at precisely regular intervals. Not only did it become certain that neutron stars - made entirely of neutrons - must exist but also, in all probability, black holes too.

The discovery was made using a newly-built radio telescope with 2048 dipole antennas. Miss Bell was a PhD student at Cambridge University. Now Mrs Jocelyn Bell Burnell, she graduated from Glasgow University in 1965. She has held research posts in three universities, and joined the Royal Observatory in Edinburgh in 1989.

See: Black Holes, Neutron.

Quantum Theory (1900)
Max Karl Ernst Ludwig Planck (1858-1947)

Max Planck, a German, suggested that just as matter is made up of particles, radiation is made up of units. One unit he called a 'quantum' (plural 'quanta'). Radiation could be absorbed only in whole numbers of quanta. The frequency of radiation, he said, is related to the quantum according to $e = hf$, where e = quantum energy, h = Planck's constant and 'f' = frequency. Planck's theory caused a scientific sensation, as it became clear that it helps to explain the behaviour of atoms, particles in atomic nuclei and electrons. It was a watershed. Physics before the theory is 'classical', after it is 'modern'. An outstanding example of its value came in 1913 when Niels Bohr (1885-1962) in Denmark incorporated quantum theory into his concept of the hydrogen atom. This explained clearly how the electrons in this atom could be thought of as circling the central nucleus in definite orbits.

Planck was born in Kiel and studied in Munich and Berlin. He joined M nich University in 1880, and later held a chair at Kiel and then Berlin. At eighty-nine he passed away in Göttingen, esteemed by the scientific world as second only to Albert Einstein.

See: Electron, Photoelectric Effect, Uncertainty Principle,
Wave Theory of Light.

Quarks (1964)

Murray Gell-Mann (1929-)

By 1962 over one hundred and fifty subatomic particles were known. To account for them, Gell-Mann formulated the concept of 'quarks'. The name came from a line in James Joyce's *Finnegan's Wake*: 'Three quarks for Muster Mark.' All protons and similar particles ('baryons') are considered to be made up of elementary particles or quarks, possessing fractional charges. There are six types or 'flavours' of quark: up, down, strange, charmed, bottom and top. Each 'flavour' has three 'colours': red, blue and green. Protons and neutrons are made up of three quarks.

In the 1980s, string theories came into favour. These do not view the basic objects as particles but as things having only length, resembling infinitely thin strings. Some time in this century it should be known if string theory represents the ultimate 'grand unified theory' of physics, if in fact such a theory is possible.

Gell-Mann became Professor of Theoretical Physics at the California Institute of Technology in 1956. His work won him the 1969 Nobel Prize for Physics.

Quasars (1963)

Maarten Schmidt (1929-)

In 1962 a faint star-like object, catalogued as 3C 273, was identified as the source of certain radio 'noise'. The spectrum of the object was puzzling and highly unusual. In 1963 Schmidt, in America, explained it as the emission lines of hydrogen subjected to a gigantic 'red shift', so big that the source had to be at a truly vast distance – 2.4 billion light years. He had found the first 'quasi-stellar object' or 'quasar'. Despite its enormous distance, 3C 273 turned out to be one of the closest quasars. It emerged that quasars are the energetic cores of active galaxies, observable at extraordinary distances because of the intensity of the radiation emitted. The energy given out by a quasar is thought to come from surrounding material falling into a supermassive black hole (one of more than about 100,000 times the mass of the Sun). The extreme shifting of spectral lines towards the red end of the spectrum is caused by the expansion of the universe. All known quasars are at great distances, so we are seeing them as they were billions of years ago. They must be ancient objects which lived out their lives in the early universe, so although we can still see them, none exist today. In the decades since the first discovery of a quasar, over 200,000 more have been found.

Schmidt was born and educated in the Netherlands. Most of his work in radio astronomy was carried out in California at the observatory on Palomar Mountain.

See: Black Holes, Expanding Universe.

Radioactivity (1896)
Antoine Henri Becquerel (1852-1908)

In 1896 Becquerel, a French physicist, wondered if the radiation from the fluorescent compound potassium uranyl sulphate contained X-rays. The substance, lying on a photographic plate wrapped in black paper, was exposed to sunlight. The ultraviolet light in this would excite the fluorescence. The results indicated X-rays were present.

Then came a spell of cloudy weather. The plates were stored in a drawer, with traces of the uranium compound on them. After some days, Becquerel ventured to develop the plates without direct sunlight. He was astounded to find that the plates were darkened by strong radiation. The 'uranic rays', as he called them, were produced continuously, whether the uranium compound was fluorescing or not. His discovery did not lead to the excitement generated by Röntgen's discovery of X-rays.

Becquerel was born in Paris and died at Le Croisie, Loire. In 1888 he obtained his doctorate, and four years later he took over a post at the Paris Museum of Natural History, one which both his grandfather and father had held.

See: - and -Rays, Artificial Radioactivity,
Isotopes, Radium and Polonium.

Radium and Polonium (1898)

Marie Curie (1867-1934) and Pierre Curie (1859-1906)

Maria Sklodowska, the youngest of five children, was born in Warsaw, Poland, which was then under Tsarist rule. At the age of fifteen she left school, after a sad childhood in which her Catholic faith faded away. From eighteen to twenty-two she worked as a governess. In 1891 she entered the University of Paris, graduating two years later in physics (top of her year), and the next year in mathematics (second in her year). In 1895 she married Pierre Curie, then a teacher at the Paris Municipal School for Industrial Physics and Chemistry. The devoted couple had two daughters, Irene (1897) and Eve (1904). The new sport of cycling was their single main relaxation from work, which tended to be their overwhelming interest.

While she was expecting Irene, Marie decided to work for a doctorate. In 1903 she presented a summary for her doctoral thesis. Probably the greatest doctoral dissertation ever, it led to her receiving two Nobel Prizes: for Physics, together with Pierre and Becquerel and later (alone) for Chemistry.

Her starting point was Becquerel's 'uranic rays'. She found that the element thorium was radioactive, and she was intrigued by pitchblende, the ore of uranium. When uranium had been removed, the ore was much more radioactive than pure uranium. Some unknown substances in the pitchblende were producing the effect. Her husband now joined her in investigating a large quantity of pitchblende. They worked hard for weeks, in primitive conditions, in a shed behind Pierre's school, driven on by their enthusiasm. Finally they discovered two highly radioactive elements; first polonium (after Poland), then radium. Seventy-five years later their notebooks were still dangerously radioactive.

After this, it took three years to obtain one decigram (0.1 g or 1/300 oz) of pure radium. This was required to confirm radium is an element, and to find the relative atomic mass. They worked with tonnes of pitchblende, in a hangar behind the school. This was bigger than the shed. However, a visitor described it as a cross between a stable and a cellar! Further work lay in investigating the properties of radioactivity.

In 1904 Pierre was made physics professor at the University of Paris. Marie – who since 1900 had been teaching at Sevres College – joined him as laboratory head. In 1906 she succeeded her husband in the physics chair, after he was killed in a traffic accident. She spent most of the First World War organising a mobile X-ray service for the French army. After this, her main role was to direct research at the Paris Radium Institute (founded in 1914). In later years she made several tours, but was often ill. In 1934 she died of leukaemia at Sancellemoz, Savoy, France.

See: - and -Rays, Artificial Radioactivity, Isotopes, Piezoelectricity and Curie Temperature.

Reflex Actions (1833)
Marshall Hall (1790-1857)

Hall, a British doctor and physiologist, discovered that reflex actions, such as dropping something very hot, are automatic and need not involve the brain. He found such actions can take place even if the connection between spinal cord and brain has been severed. His experiments were carried out on dogs, rabbits and other small mammals.

In 1812 Hall qualified in Edinburgh as a physician. Born in Basford, near Stoke-on-Trent, he was a cotton manufacturer's son. His first practice was in Nottingham, but in 1826 he moved to London. Thirty-one years later he suffered a fatal illness in Brighton.

Reflex Arcs (1906)

Sir Charles Scott Sherrington (1857-1952)

In 1891 Sherrington commenced work at the University of London, into spinal reflexes. From experiments on animals from which most of the brains had been removed, he showed that reflex actions do not require thought. The body contains a coordinated system of 'reflex arcs'. Suppose a person is handed a very hot plate. Via an in-built reflex arc, sensory nerves transmit a message, through intermediate neurones in the spinal cord, directly to motor nerves, which operate arm muscles to drop the plate. The action takes place very rapidly, protecting the body. Doctors sometimes partially check the general integrity of the nervous system by the patellar reflex or 'knee jerk' (first noted in 1875 by the German, Otto Westphal).

Sherrington, a Londoner, studied medicine at Cambridge. In 1895 he became Professor of Physiology at Liverpool. His pioneering work on reflexes was carried out in the first few years of the twentieth century. In 1920 he became President of the Royal Society. He retired to Eastbourne, where he died peacefully at the age of ninety-five.

See: Reflex Actions.

Relativity Theories (1905 & 1915)

Albert Einstein (1879-1955)

When he was fourteen, Einstein asked himself what the world would look like if he could ride on a light beam. Twelve years later came his famous paper *On the Electrodynamics of Moving Bodies*. This set out the special theory of relativity, which ignores gravity. Its basis is that the laws of science are all the same for all freely-moving observers, regardless of their motion.

Significant consequences are that the universe's only constant measure is 'c', the speed of light in a vacuum; that 'c', the greatest speed possible, is the same the all observers; and energy and mass are equivalent. The last point led to the well-known equation $E = mc^2$, E being the quantity of energy obtained on destroying a mass m.

In 1915 came his second theory of the nature of matter, space and time - the general theory of relativity. In this, the force of gravity is not seen as similar to other forces, but is explained in terms of the curvature of space-time. It took time for relativity theory to be widely accepted, as several of its predictions seemed to contradict common sense: eg the velocity of light in a vacuum is the same for all observers, regardless of their own movements; when the speed of an object increases, its mass increases and its length decreases; light is bent by gravitational force; time seems to go more slowly near a planet or other massive object. Experiments during the twentieth century indicated that Einstein was right, eg according to Einstein, an intense gravitational field slows down atomic vibrations, shown by a shift of spectral lines towards the red. This 'Einstein shift' was found in the spectra of white dwarf stars and even in the spectrum of the Sun.

Einstein was born in Ulm in southern Germany, but soon

afterwards the family moved to Munich. Being Jewish, the family was isolated in a city of Catholics. Einstein's headmaster prophesied that the boy would 'never make a success of anything'. In 1894 his father's business in electrical engineering failed and Einstein soon followed the rest of the family to Milan. At a second attempt, he was accepted as a student at the polytechnic school in Z rich. In 1900 he graduated with an enthusiasm for physics rather than engineering. In 1905 he became a Swiss citizen, two years after he had married Mileva, a Hungarian lady who had been studying mathematics in Switzerland. From 1902-1909 he worked as a patent examiner at the Berne Patent Office. In 1905 he published not only the paper about his special theory but two other fundamentally significant papers, one explaining Brownian motion, the other the photoelectric effect. The paper on photoelectricity won him the 1921 Nobel Prize for Physics.

In 1909 Einstein went to Z rich University, moving two years later to the German University in Prague and in 1914 to Berlin. He resumed German nationality. In 1919 he was divorced. His ex-wife and two sons were then back in Z rich. When he was ill he was looked after by his cousin, Elsa, and they soon married. He grew to despise the regimented and aggressive atmosphere of Germany. In 1933, when Hitler came to power, Einstein was in the USA, and decided to remain there. In 1940 he became an American citizen. Although a pacifist, he helped in the making of the first atomic bomb, as he was concerned that Nazi scientists would make one first.

In later life, he further developed the general theory of relativity and attempted to discover a theory unifying electromagnetic and gravitational fields.

See: Big Bang, Brownian Motion, Photoelectric Effect,
Quantum Theory, Riemannian Geometry, Space-Time Continuum.

Riemannian Geometry (1854)

Georg Friedrich Bernhard Riemann (1826-1866)

Euclid's thirteen-volume 'Elements' has been called the greatest set of textbooks ever. They contain little original work, but are a compendium of two-dimensional geometry, accepted as correct for hundreds of years. In 1854 Riemann put forward the principal form of non-Euclidean geometry. This is based partly on axioms different from those of Euclid, eg more than one line parallel to a given line can be drawn through a given point, and through two points any number of straight lines can be drawn. The consequences can be surprising to someone steeped in Euclid's theorems, for example the angles of a triangle do not necessarily add up to 180°. If a triangle is not flat but drawn, for example, on the surface of a sphere, or the Earth, the sum of its angles is over 180°. Riemann's work is geometry generalised for any number of dimensions and situations. Einstein acknowledged this as superior to traditional geometry, which is restricted to flat figures.

Riemann was horn at Breselenz, near Hanover, Germany, the second of six children born to a Lutheran pastor. In 1848 his college career was interrupted by army service for the Prussian king during a revolution. Three years later he obtained a doctorate at Göttingen. His brilliant pioneering studies in mathematics were ended by tuberculosis. Probably he would have gone on to other important work in mathematics or philosophy. As it was, he made some astonishing suggestions, such as saying space may be curved into a closed ball. Years before Einstein's birth he was anticipating an aspect of relativity theory in which the curvature of space-time was a key concept.

Riemann's widest fame today is as the originator of the Riemann Hypothesis, considered the most significant unproven mathematical conjecture. It purports to describe the distribution of the prime numbers, a mathematical Holy Grail which has been sought for centuries without success. The predictions of the Riemann Hypothesis have been tested as correct out to prime numbers in the trillions, but that is not the same as proving the hypothesis.

Riemann's disease ended his life when he was only forty, in the town of Selasca, Italy.

See: Relativity Theories, Space-Time Continuum.

Rockets (about 1150 AD)

The Chinese military

We know the rocket was invented in China, but we do not know by whom. From the 10th century AD, following the Chinese invention of gunpowder in the 9th century, military forces in China developed an array of fearsome weapons, which included bombs, cannons, crossbows, fireworks, flame-throwers, flares, guns of several kinds, mines (land and sea), poison gas, smoke bombs and stink bombs, as well as rockets. It is on record that over the years the Chinese soldiers used every poisonous or evil-smelling substance they could think of; a particularly disgusting example is the 'excrement bomb', which consisted of dried human excrement, poisonous wolfsbane, croton oil, soap-bean pods (to produce black smoke), arsenious oxide, Cantharid beetles and tung oil.

The first rockets were intended purely for warfare. They were first used about 1150, and later versions resembled the notorious

V1 rockets of World War II. The modern use of rockets to propel men and probes into space may mean that the rocket has been China's most important technological contribution to the world.

Rotation of the Earth (350 BC)
Heraclides of Ponticus (388-315 BC)

The Greek philosopher Heraclides was the first to suppose that the Earth rotates on its axis. To him this seemed a logical way of explaining day and night. Most ancient thinkers had doubts, which were to persist for over two thousand years. In 1632 the Inquisition in Rome forced Galileo to recant his belief in a moving Earth, although it is said he muttered to himself, 'Even so, it does move'. He was thinking particularly of support for Copernicus's view that the Earth is a planet circling the Sun.

Proof of our rotating planet was given in 1851 by the French scientist Jean Foucault. He set a very long pendulum swinging from the dome of a Paris church. This maintained its swing in a fixed plane, independent of the Earth's motion. Observations over several days showed that the Earth was turning round. From time to time, Foucault's experiment has been repeated for public viewing at the Science Museum, London.

Heraclides was horn at Heraclea Eregli, on the Black Sea shore. He went to Athens when a young man, and spent some years in Plato's Academy. The remainder of his life was mostly spent in Athens, where he died at the age of seventy-three.

See: Jupiter's Satellites and Law of Falling Bodies.

S

Sahara Desert from Italy (AD 42)

Suetonius Paulinus (AD 6-62)

In AD 42 the Roman Paulinus crossed the Atlas Mountains and
entered the Sahara. On his return he received much acclaim, but
others were not inspired to explore. No one thought there was
more to Africa than mountains and desert.

Salvarsan (1909)

Paul Ehrlich (1854-1915)

Following the identification by Robert Koch and others of bacteria
causing particular diseases, Ehrlich set out to find drugs to kill the
germs. Interest in synthetic dyes which stain bacteria led him to a
red dye that stains trypanosomes, the cause of sleeping sickness. He
found it moderately effective in killing the organism, and tried to
make stronger derivatives by introducing arsenic into the structure.
In 1909 one of his students, Sahachiro Hata, came across a
compound that had little effect on trypanosomes hut was deadly
against the bacteria causing syphilis. 'Compound 606' (the six
hundred and sixth substance to be tested) became known as
'arsphenamine' or 'Salvarsan', meaning 'safe arsenic'. In fact it was
not particularly safe, but it was the first synthetic drug.

Ehrlich devoted the rest of his life to curing syphilis using Salvarsan. He had pioneered chemotherapy, in which drugs are used to attack diseases. This approach proved highly successful, notably with sulphanilamide (1933) and other 'sulpha' drugs. These were wonderfully effective against bacterial diseases, but soon were surpassed by penicillin, streptomycin, aureomycin and the many other antibiotics.

See: Bacteriological Techniques, Penicillin.

Scurvy - Prevention and Cure (1747)
James Lind (1716-1794)

In early times, sailors on long voyages ate mainly hard tack and salted pork. Scurvy, caused by vitamin C deficiency, often struck men down, but its cause was then a mystery. In 1747 Lind, a Scottish physician, sailed as surgeon on HMS *Salisbury*. Eighty of the crew of three hundred and fifty had scurvy. Lind divided twelve sufferers into six pairs, five of which had to drink five potions daily. The potions were different – cider, dilute vitriol, sea water, vinegar and a herbal mixture, The sixth pair had two oranges and a lemon. Within a week, these last two men were well enough to look after the others.

The discovery was published in *Treatise of the Scurvy* in 1753, but it took forty-two years for the British Admiralty to respond. One year after Lind's death, sailors were ordered to take lemon or lime juice daily, and scurvy was prevented. The practice led to the expression 'limey' for a British sailor, and to 'Limehouse' for the London district where the limes were stored. Lind obtained his doctor's degree at Edinburgh after his 1747 voyage. In 1783 he was appointed physician to King George III.

See: Beriberi Prevention and Cure, Vitamins.

Sequence of Amino Acids in Proteins (1953) and of Nucleotides in DNA (1984)

Frederick Sanger (1918-2013)

Sanger was the first person to win two Nobel Prizes for Chemistry. His first prize (1958) was for discovering the structure of insulin. This is a protein with two chains in the molecule, one a chain of thirty amino acids, the other a chain of twenty-one. Using a reagent that would attach itself to the end of a chain, he was able to peel off some amino acids one by one, identifying each end-product by paper chromatography. Other techniques were used to break a chain into fragments which could be analysed. It took eight years to decipher the precise order of the amino acids, and to ascertain the small differences between human, sheep, horse, pig and whale insulin.

Biochemists were quick to adopt Sanger's procedures. By 1960 the tobacco mosaic virus structure (one hundred and fifty-eight amino acids) was known and by 1964, the two hundred and twenty-three amino acids of trypsin, an enzyme, had been deciphered. In 1967 P. Edman, in Australia, designed his 'sequenator', which utilised an automated technique to ascertain the sequence of units in proteins.

Already Sanger's work was incredibly useful, but he went on to discover ways of determining the sequence of nucleotides in DNA, ie the chemical structures of genes. By 1984 his team had found the sequence of 150,000 nucleotides comprising the entire genetic constitution of certain viruses. This work won him the second Nobel Prize, shared with two Americans, P. Berg and W. Gilbert.

Sanger was an Englishman who graduated from Cambridge

University in 1939. He worked at Cambridge and, from 1951, at the Medical Research Council laboratories.

See: Amino Acids, DNA and RNA, Insulin.

Sex Chromosomes (1907)

Thomas Hunt Morgan (1866-1945)

Morgan, an American zoologist, selected fruit flies for genetic research. The fruit fly breeds prolifically and rapidly, needs little food and has only four pairs of chromosomes. It was found that in a male fly, one chromosome pair consists of a normal sized or X chromosome, and a smaller or Y chromosome. In the female the corresponding pair is two identical X chromosomes. In fertilisation, one chromosome from the male's XY pair fuses with one from the female's XX, producing a male (XY) or a female (XX). This mechanism operates in all sexually reproducing organisms, although sometimes, especially in some species of birds, the female is XY.

Sex chromosome abnormality can lead to character traits, eg XYY males seem irrational and short-tempered. A sex-linked disease, eg haemophilia or colour-blindness in males, is now known to be due to a defective X chromosome paired with the Y chromosome.

Morgan was horn at Lexington, Kentucky. Graduating in 1886, he obtained a doctorate four years later, and in 1904 obtained the Chair in Experimental Zoology at Columbia. His 1926 work *The Theory Of The Gene* extended Mendel's pioneering work in genetics as far as the microscope would allow. He won a Nobel Prize in 1933, and died twelve years later in Pasadena, California.

See: Laws of Heredity.

Sex Hormones (1923)

Edgar Allen (1892-1943) and Edward Adelbert Doisy
(1893-1987)

In France, in 1889, seventy-two year old Dr Brown-Sequard pronounced himself rejuvenated after injections of an extract containing ground-up animal testes. Within weeks, patent medicines containing such extracts were on sale. It was not until the early 1920s that investigations had any success. In 1923 Allen found that spayed mice went into heat if injected with fluid from pig ovaries. Arguing that a female hormone is present in the fluid, he worked with a friend, biochemist Edward Doisy, to concentrate the fluid. This proved difficult, but they then heard of the work of Selmar Aschheim and Bernard Zondek, two Berlin gynaecologists. Searching for a clear method of diagnosing pregnancy, they had found that urine from a pregnant woman, injected into an immature mouse or rat, made the animal go into heat. It was clear that a pregnant mammal has a female sex hormone in its urine. In 1929 Allen and Doisy isolated 'oestrin', soon found to be one of a family, the oestrogens. Five years later, a quite separate hormone, progesterone, was isolated from the corpus luteum.

In Germany, Adolf Butenandt also isolated oestrin, and in 1931 he obtained the first male sex hormone, testosterone from 25,000 litres (5,500 gallons) of urine. Four years later the pure hormone was obtained in Amsterdam from bull testes.

Allen and Doisy Worked at Washington University, in St Louis, Missouri, USA. They became friends after playing baseball together. Doisy, with other colleagues, was later the first to isolate vitamin K, involved in the clotting of blood. He became Professor of

Biochemistry at St Louis in 1923, the year in which cooperation with Dr Allen began.

South American Interior (1799-1804) and Biogeography (1806)

Friedrich Heinrich Alexander von Humboldt (1769-1859)

This explorer, biologist and geologist focused attention on the significance of scientific explanation in natural history. He developed the science of biogeography, which studies the distribution of living things. His work was a major influence on Charles Darwin and Alfred Wallace, who independently initiated our concepts of evolution. In his lifetime Humboldt was second only to Napoleon in fame.

His birthplace was Berlin, capital of Prussia. He and Wilhelm, his brother, were taught privately before studying together at Göttingen University. Here he met Georg Forster, who had journeyed with Captain Cook. In 1790 the two made a grand tour of Europe. The next year Humboldt entered a leading geological institute at Freiberg, Saxony, headed by Abraham Werner, a pioneer of rock classification.

In 1799 he sailed with a French naturalist, Aimé Bonpland, to explore Spanish colonies in South America. The next year they left Caracas to investigate the river plains of Venezuela and the Orinoco, traveling on foot, on horseback and by canoe. Humboldt saw much to astonish, including the preparation of curare as a paralytic agent, the catching of electric eels and evidence of cannibalism. After showing that the Casiquiare Canal joins the Amazon headwaters to those of the Orinoco they turned back, taking sixty thousand plant specimens, over a tenth of which had not been seen before in Europe. Next they visited Cuba, Peru, Colombia and Ecuador. From Quito they climbed Chimborazo, then the highest mountain known, and were the first to realise that oxygen shortage causes mountain sickness. They saw Lima, then spent a year exploring Mexico before returning to Europe in 1804.

In 1807 Humboldt was sent as a Prussian delegate to Paris, where he settled tor twenty years. In that period he wrote up his epic travels and with the chemist Gay-Lussac (1778-1350), showed that air from anywhere always has the same composition. He returned to Berlin in 1827, and two years later travelled to Russia at the Tsar's invitation. He visited the Urals, then pressed on through Siberia to the border with China. In later years he studied the Earth's magnetism, and completed Kosmos, a five-volume history of science and description of the universe. He died at ninety in poverty, leaving all personal possessions to his servant, who sold his famous library and notes for a trifle.

See: Natural Selection.

Space-Time Continuum (1907)

Hermann Minkowski (1864-1909)

Minkowski, a Russian-born German mathematician, was one of Einstein's teachers. He realised that Einstein's view of the universe interrelated space and time, so that either concept on its own is without real meaning. We need to recognise four dimensions - length, breadth, height and time. Minkowski suggested that the four-dimensional fusion be known as the 'space-time continuum'. According to relativity theory, space-time is curved or 'warped' by the distribution of matter and energy.

Minkowski was born in Alexota, Russia. His higher education was in Germany, where he obtained a doctorate (Königsberg, 1885). When he was forty-five he suffered a fatal heart attack at Göttingen. *See: Big Bang, Relativity Theories.*

Structure of Nucleic Acids (1953)

Francis Harry Compton Crick (1916-2004) and James Dewey Watson (1928-)

By 1950 much information had been recorded about DNA and RNA. In 1951 Linus Pauling and others in America suggested that proteins can have a helical structure, like a spiral staircase. Crick and Watson reviewed all the data, and then came up with the idea that a nucleic acid molecule is a double helix, with two sugar-phosphate backbones winding up a common vertical axis. From each sugar-phosphate chain, purines and pyrimidines extend across, like the steps of a ladder. The Watson-Crick model is very successful in explaining the properties of nucleic acids, eg genetic coding is due to the precise combinations of purines and pyrimidines. The discovery is generally considered the most significant biological discovery of the twentieth century, and has revolutionised the science of genetics.

Most of the work on DNA was done at the Cavendish Laboratory, Cambridge, by Crick, an English molecular biologist, and Watson, his US colleague. In 1962 they were awarded the Nobel Prize, together with Maurice Wilkins, a New Zealand biophysicist. Wilkins, working at King's College, London, had helped in elucidating the structure. A colleague of his, Rosalind Franklin, would also have shared the Nobel Prize, but she died in

1958 from cancer at the age of thirty-eight. She had produced X-ray diffraction photographs of DNA indicating that the structure is indeed helical.

See: DNA and RNA.

Sun is the Centre of the Solar System (240 BC)
Aristarchus of Samos (3rd century BC)

The Alexandrian Aristarchus was the most daring of Greek astronomers. Realising that the Sun was larger than the Earth, he taught that our planet orbits the Sun. For hundreds of years the favoured view had been that the Earth was the centre of the universe, as laid down by Aristotle (384-322 BC) and Ptolemy (127-148). In 1543 the Polish priest Nicolaus Copernicus (1473-1543) published a book arguing convincingly that Aristarchus' view was right. It took nearly a century for the Copernican system to be accepted, even though it was supported by Galileo.

See: Distance of Moon from Earth and Precession of the Equinoxes, Jupiter's Satellites and Law of Falling Bodies.

Superconductivity (1911)
Heike Kamerlingh Onnes (1853-1926)

Kamerlingh Onnes, a Dutch physicist, was the first person lo liquefy helium, in 1908. Three years later he discovered 'super-conductivity', finding that at 4° above absolute zero mercury had zero electrical resistance. A lead ring at 7° above absolute zero maintained a current within it for two and a half years. Studies of superconductivity continue today but always the temperature has to be extremely low. Today superconducting magnets are some of the most powerful electromagnets known and future applications are expected to include electrical power transmission, power storage devices and refrigeration.

See: Helium.

Superfluidity (1935)

Willem Hendrik Keesom (1876-1956) and Anna Keesom (1883-1960)

In 1935 Willem Keesom and his sister were studying helium at very low temperatures They were working in the Onnes laboratory in Leiden when they discovered that liquid helium at temperatures close to absolute zero conducts heat almost perfectly. Studies by a Russian, Peter Kapitza, showed that this is because it flows extraordinarily easily. Its viscosity is one thousandth that of hydrogen gas. Superfluid helium forms a film on glass and will flow as fast as it pours.

Supernovae (1885)

Ernst Hartwig (1851-1923)

Following the invention of the telescope, a remarkable nova, or 'new star', was discovered by Hartwig in Germany. The star was located in the nearby Andromeda galaxy and came to be known as S Andromedae. Many other novae had been discovered previously, but when Hubble deduced its distance, it was realised that this new object was ten thousand times brighter than a normal nova.

Many more of these superbright novae have since been found, and they are now classed as supernovae. Supernovae and novae are actually quite different phenomena; a supernova explodes because its core collapses, and all that is left is a massive core or even a black hole. A nova is observed when a white dwarf star explodes because of a critical increase in mass caused by the accretion of hydrogen on to its surface from a companion star; the white dwarf survives the event.

Supernovae are frequently spotted among the stars of the millions of other visible galaxies, but are only very occasionally observed in our own (the Milky Way), eg in 1006, 1054, 1572 and 1604; none has been recorded here since 1604, and S Andromedae was the closest supernova to Earth seen in the last four hundred years (although many are thought to go unrecorded because they are obscured by galactic matter).

See: Black Holes.

Synthetic Dyes (1856)

Sir William Henry Perkin (1838-1907)

At the age of seventeen Perkin became an assistant at the Royal College of Science, London. He worked on coal tar compounds, and soon had his own home laboratory. Here in 1856, when trying to synthesise quinine, he accidentally obtained a beautiful purple colour. A Scottish firm found it useful as a dyestuff. Perkin patented it, and rapidly became rich as the manufacturer of 'mauveine', the first synthetic dye. Other chemists, inspired by Perkin, soon found how to make similar products. After a time, many producers of natural dyes were put out of business by the fast-growing synthetic dye industry. At the age of 35 Perkin retired from business to concentrate on research. In 1875 he synthesised coumarin, a natural product smelling of newly-cut hay. This success was the start of the synthetic perfume industry.

Perkin was born in London and became a hard-working pupil, fascinated by chemistry. He was knighted only a year before his death in Sudbury, Suffolk, at the age of sixty-nine.

T

Tasmania, New Zealand, Tonga and Fiji from Netherlands (1642-1643)

Abel Janszoon Tasman (1603-1659)

Tasman was horn in Groningen in the Netherlands. He went to sea as an ordinary seaman, but by 1635 was a junior admiral. On his main voyage, from 1642-1643, he explored the Southern Indian Ocean. First to be reached was Tasmania, which he did not identify as an island; he named it Van Diemen's Land in honour of the Governor-General of the Dutch East Indies, the man who had sent Tasman on his mission. Sailing on, Tasman came to New Zealand, which he thought to be part of an 'unknown south land'. Travelling on north-east, he discovered the islands of Tonga and Fiji. Tasman was unlucky - he had sailed around Australia without seeing it.

He was also unlucky in love. When he returned to Amsterdam in 1637, his wife cut him out of her will. Later he married again, but the union was not a happy one.

In 1644 his second major expedition explored parts of the Australian coast, reaching 'New Holland' (Western Australia), which had been discovered by other Dutch mariners. He ended up as a merchant in Jakarta (then Batavia), where he died.

See: Australia from Netherlands, Pacific Islands from England.

Thermoelectricity (1823)
Thomas Johann Seebeck (1770-1831)

Seebeck, a German physicist, found that if two metals are linked in an electrical circuit and heat is applied to the junction of the metals, a current flows. This effect is utilised in devices such as the thermoelectric thermometer and thermoelectric cell.

Seebeck was born in Reval, Estonia, but most of his work was done in Berlin. The poet Goethe was a friend, and for a time they worked together in attempts to explain colours. Seebeck's only discovery of note was the thermoelectric effect. Little use of this was made for more than one hundred years, until semiconductor devices became important.

Timbuktu from England (1826)
Alexander Gordon Laing (1793-1826)

Laing is said to have been the first European to see Timbuktu (Tombouctou), which is in Mali, West Africa. Of the principal 'forbidden cities' – Lhasa, Mecca and Timbuktu – it was the last to be visited from Europe. In 1822, when he was serving with the British Army in Sierra Leone, Laing was sent inland, and then in 1825 he set out to explore the Niger river. Eventually he got to Timbuktu, wounded badly by Tuareg nomads. He stayed in the 'untainted' city for a month, only to be killed by Tuaregs two days into the journey back. The first Westerner to see the Muslim city and return was a Frenchman, Rene-Auguste Caillié (1828).

Tracers (1904)

Franz Knoop (1875-1946)

In 1904 Knoop, a German biochemist, fed labelled fats to dogs in an attempt to see what happened to the digested fats. The 'labels' were benzene rings at one end of the fat molecules. Benzene was used because no mammal has enzymes to decompose it. The benzene was found always to turn up in the dogs' urine attached to a 2-carbon atom side chain. This showed that the body splits off the carbon atoms in a fat molecule two at a time. Knoop had carried out the first successful 'tracing' in biochemistry.

The use of radioisotopes as tracers, started in 1913 by a Hungarian, George Charles de Hevesy, became highly successful in tracing the fates of substances absorbed by plants and animals.

Tutankhamun's Tomb (1922)

Howard Carter (1874-1939)

Carter, a British archaeologist, spent several seasons searching in the Valley of the Kings near Luxor, Egypt. In November 1922 his team came across the tomb of the eighteen-year-old Pharaoh Tutankhamun. The mummified body was in poor condition, but the tomb contained many intact treasures. They had lain undisturbed since 1323 BC, whereas the tombs of other Pharaohs had been damaged and plundered long ago.

Tutankhamun had been buried hastily, and the priests had not laid a curse on anyone disturbing the site. The myth of the curse probably arose from the death in 1923 of the Earl of Carnarvon, who had sponsored Carter's excavations.

Ultrasonics (1915)
Paul Langevin (1872-1946)

Langevin, a French physicist, discovered in 1915 that crystals could be made to vibrate so quickly that they produced ultrasonic waves (frequencies higher than the upper limit of human hearing). He made use of Pierre and Jacques Curie's 1880 discovery of piezoelectricity, and went on to develop the underwater equivalent of radar – 'sonar' (sound navigation and ranging). Ultrasonic diagnostic techniques have become a useful tool in modern medicine.

Langevin, a Parisian, studied at Cambridge under Sir J.J. Thomson, and then at the Sorbonne under Pierre Curie. In 1904 he was appointed Professor of Physics at the College de France. Later he became politically active and a vehement opponent of Nazism.
See: Echo-sounding by Bats, Piezoelectricity.

Uncertainty Principle (1927)
Werner Heisenberg (1901-1976)

Heisenberg, a German physicist, asked a profound question which projected particle physics into an almost unknowable realm – how do we know the exact position of a particle such as an electron?

He was led to put forward the principle of uncertainty, according to which it is impossible to know precisely both a particle's position and its velocity. The more accurately the one is known, the less accurately is the other. Heisenberg saw that the very act of trying to measure something very precisely changes its value. The phenomenon is seen in everyday life, eg when a gauge is used to find the air pressure in a tyre, it lets out a little air, altering the pressure. Such a change is tiny and insignificant. With subatomic particles, however, the effect is large and highly significant.

Based on Heisenberg's principle, a new theory, quantum mechanics, led to particles like electrons being treated in terms of wave and particle properties. The theory is based on a new type of mathematics. As yet it has not proved possible to unify it with the general theory of relativity, which is concerned with the large-scale structure of the universe.

Heisenberg was born in Duisberg, and obtained a PhD in Munich in 1923. His research concerned atomic theory, and it was years before philosophers appreciated the significance of the uncertainty principle and the limit it puts on human knowledge. During the Second World War Heisenberg was in charge of German research into atomic weapons.

See: Electron, Quantum Theory, Relativity Theories.

Uniformitarianism (1821)

Sir Charles Lyell (1797-1875)

Lyell was a Scottish barrister. His three-volume treatise *Principles of Geology* had eleven editions in his lifetime alone. The books held that geological truth must be found by strictly adhering to 'uniformitarianism', a methodology that takes the present as the key to the past. It notes the uniformity of natural forces acting in a process of slow, unending change. Lyell's writings showed that all geological events can be produced by causes operating over millions of years. His work was given attention by Darwin in his studies of South American landscapes. They were close friends.

Lyell's birthplace was Kinnordy, Angus, Scotland. He graduated from Oxford in 1819 and began a career in law, already intrigued by geology.

See: Plutonic Theory of Earth's Origin.

V

Vitamins (1912)
Casimir Funk (1884-1967)

Scurvy was well known in the ancient world and proved a hazard on long sea voyages. In 1536 Jacques Cartier, a French explorer, was wintering in Canada. Many of his crew were dying from scurvy, until they adopted a suggestion from local Indians to drink plenty of water in which pine needles had been soaked. Some of the sailors considered that they had been cured by magic. In 1747 Lind found how to prevent scurvy, and in 1891 Takaki had success against beriberi. Five years later Eijkman proved that this disease can be cured by diet. At the time no one could explain the victories over scurvy and beriberi.

The need for trace chemicals to maintain life became clear in 1905. Pekelharing in the Netherlands found that mice could not survive on an artificial diet that contained adequate carbohydrates, proteins, fats and water unless they also received a few drops of fresh milk daily. The next year, in England, Hopkins got similar results with rats, and declared that mammals need 'accessory food factors'. Six years later Funk, working at the Lister Institute in London, isolated the substance in rice husks that prevents beriberi in pigeons. The compound turned out to be in the class of compounds called amines, and he called it a 'vitamine' ('life amine' in Latin). He suggested that beriberi, scurvy, pellagra and rickets all arise from deficiencies of 'vitamines'. This was found to be true, and soon other deficiency diseases were identified. In 1920 the name 'vitamin' was adopted when it had become clear that most of the compounds are not amines.

Funk was born in Warsaw, qualified in Berne as a doctor, then worked in Paris, Berlin and London. In 1915 he went to America and was naturalised five years later. 1923 saw him back in Warsaw, but he returned to the USA for good at the outbreak of the Second World War (1939).

See: Beriberi Prevention and Cure, Scurvy Prevention and Cure.

W

Wave Theory of Light (1678)
Christiaan Huygens (1629-1695)

Huygens, a Dutch astronomer, proposed in 1678 that light consists of tiny waves, not tiny particles as Newton thought. The wave theory explains why refraction (bending) of light varies with colour (which depends on wavelength) and how two beams can cross without affecting each other. On the other hand, Newton's view explains why light travels in straight lines and casts sharp shadows. For about a century Newton's view was accepted, ignoring the problem that beams of particles could not cross without collisions occurring. The wave theory was rejected, in part because light reaches us across empty space, and it was then believed that all waves require a medium (a substance to travel through). In 1801 Young's interference experiments led to the adoption of the wave theory. Today we accept that light is waves of one form of electromagnetic radiation, which travel in 'quanta' (bursts or 'packets' of energy).

Huygens was born in The Hague and died there. His education at the University of Leiden stimulated an interest in mathematics, and in 1657 he produced the first formal work on probability. About this time he devised a good way of grinding lenses for telescopes, which led him to make various astronomical discoveries,

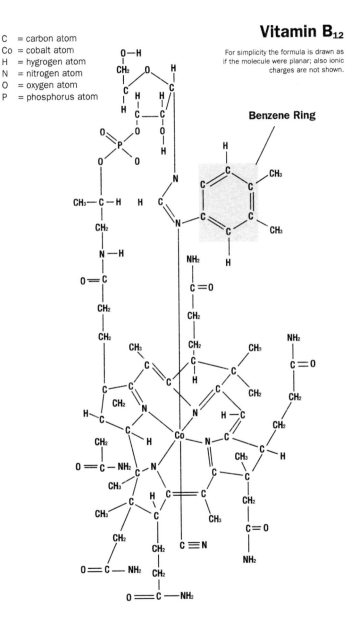

Vitamin B₁₂

C = carbon atom
Co = cobalt atom
H = hygrogen atom
N = nitrogen atom
O = oxygen atom
P = phosphorus atom

For simplicity the formula is drawn as
if the molecule were planar; also ionic
charges are not shown.

Benzene Ring

some using a telescope 7 m (23 ft) long. He is also remembered as the inventor of the pendulum clock.

See: Electromagnetic Waves, Gravitation, Laws of Motion and Dispersion of White Light, Interference, Quantum Theory.

Witwatersrand Gold Deposits (1886)

George Harrison

The Witwatersrand ('Ridge of White Waters') is a long outcrop in South Africa containing vast deposits of gold. The discoverer, a prospector called George Harrison, sold his claim for ten pounds in 1886. His affidavit – to the Department of Mines in Pretoria – led to a massive gold rush, and to the development of Johannesburg as a major city.

World Wide Web (1969)

Sir Tim Berners-Lee OM, KBC, FRS, FREng, FRSA, DFBCS, (1955-)

Berners-Lee majored in physics at Queen's College Oxford and while an undergraduate he made a computer using spare parts. When he was caught hacking, he was banned from using the college computers. After graduating in 1976 he worked on a number of programming projects before becoming a software engineer for CERN, the vast particle physics laboratory on the French/Swiss border. It was at CERN that he developed the initial prototype for the Web.

He began to work on distributed real-time systems for acquisition of scientific data, and visualised a global information space with computers linked around the planet. The linking would enable researchers to 'surf' from one body of data to another both obtaining information and sharing thoughts and insights with others. In 1989 he sent a proposal to CERN, but received no response.

Making use of work done in 1945 by Vannevar Bush and later efforts by Ted Nelson and Doug Engelbart, Berners-Lee came up with the hypertext transfer protocol or HTTP, a language computers could use to communicate via a network. He also envisaged a unique address called the Universal Resource Identifier – the URL. In 1990 he produced the first 'browser' or client program for viewing documents; he called this the 'www'. Berners-Lee wrote the first web server, software to deal with the storing and transmission of web pages. Then he created HTML, a language for describing the form and layout of matter on a page and went on to set up the first web server, info.cern.ch. In 1991 the www browser and web server became available on the Internet, advertised through various news groups.

Berners-Lee was determined to keep the web available to everyone and free of patents or royalties. The number of users soon skyrocketed and in 1994 he set up the WWW Consortium.

He became the first holder of the 3-com Founder's Chair at the Massachusetts Institute of Technology (MIT), where he became a senior research scientist. He has since been made a Distinguished Fellow of the British Computer Society, a member of the US Aacdemy of Arts and Sciences and a Fellow of the Royal Society, and in 2004 he was knighted. A 'fiercely protective' family man who gives few interviews, he is thought to have a net worth over 50m dollars.

Wreck of the Titanic (1985)

Robert Ballard (1943-) and Jean-Louis Michel (1949-)

In the early hours of April 15 1912, the 52,000-ton Royal Mail Ship *Titanic* sank after hitting an iceberg 400 miles south of Newfoundland on the fifth day of her maiden transatlantic voyage. Of the 2227 people on board, 1522 were lost, having either drowned or died from exposure in the icy sea. For many decades after the tragedy the technology to locate, let alone salvage, the wreck in more than two miles of water did not exist, although there were plenty of outlandish suggestions, from filling the wreck with ping pong balls to turning it into an iceberg. In the early 1980s a series of expeditions to locate it were funded by Jack Grimm, an eccentric Texas oil entrepreneur.

Success finally came in 1985 to a Franco-American search team sponsored by the US Navy and led by Robert Ballard and Jean-Louis Michel of the French National Institute of Oceanography, based in Paris. After a series of fruitless sonar sweeps of the search area, Ballard and Michel realised it would be more effective to use the ship's cameras to search for items of debris from the ship than to rely on sonar, and as a result of this change in tactics the wreck was finally found and photographed in the early hours of September 1 1985 at a depth of 3784m (12,415ft); it turned out that the *Titanic* had broken in two at the surface and the two halves had struck the sea bed a third of a mile apart. The next year, Ballard landed a submersible on the Titanic's decks, and investigation has continued since.

Ballard had left California in 1967 to join the Woods Hole Oceanographic Institution, Massachusetts, as a navy ensign. After leaving the Navy, he remained with the Institution as an underwater geologist, gaining a PhD in 1974. Both the Woods Hole Oceanographic Institution and the French National Institute of Oceanography provided back-up for the search, which lasted over five weeks and used advanced sonar apparatus and deep-water visual imaging technology.

X-Rays (1895)
Wilhelm Konrad von Röntgen (1845-1923)

Wilhelm Röntgen was working with cathode rays (electron beams) in W rzberg, Germany, in 1895. To his amazement, he saw that a screen coated in a fluorescent compound was glowing, although the discharge tube was covered with black paper. Inside the evacuated tube the cathode rays were striking a metal plate, which was emitting mysterious rays, 'X-rays' as he called them. Rontgen discovered that the rays would penetrate wood, rubber, flesh and other opaque materials. His intense fascination was soon shared by many. Physicist Ernest Rutherford, at the time a Cambridge research student, wrote to his fiancée that his professor (J.J. Thomson) was '...trying to find out the real cause of the waves, and the great object is to find the theory before anyone else, for nearly every professor in Europe is now on the warpath'. By 30th April 1896, the journal *Nature* alone had printed over one hundred and fifty articles about the rays.

Röntgen was a German-born Dutchman. He did not do well at school, and had difficulty in getting a place at Z rich Polytechnic, In 1888 he was appointed to the chair in physics at W rzberg University.

See: Electromagnetic Waves.

Z

Zimbabwe's Ruins from England (1891)
James Theodore Bent (1852-1897)

Bent, a British archaeologist, explored and documented massive ruins in Zimbabwe in Southern Africa. The country was then an English colony, Southern Rhodesia, which after independence became the state of Zimbabwe. The ancient and mysterious ruins are described in Bent's work *The Ruined Cities of Mashonaland*. With his wife Mabel, Bent made expeditions to other parts of Africa, to southern Arabia and to Turkey.

Zone Refining (1952)
William Gardner Pfann (1919-1982)

A breakthrough in electronics, the transistor was invented in 1947. To be efficient, transistors must be made of extraordinarily pure materials. At just the right time, Pfann, a US chemical engineer, found a way of achieving such purity in semiconductors such as germanium or silicon. A rod to be treated |s slowly pulled through the hollow of a circular heater, so the melted part travels along it. Most impurities stay in the melted zone and accumulate at one end of the rod, while others tend to remain at the other end. The process is repeated several times, until the bulk of the material has almost no foreign particles. Dr Pfann discovered the technique in California whilst trying to obtain ultra-pure germanium. Later it was found that pretreatment is necessary to remove certain impurities, especially boron. The purified rods are 'doped' with tiny amounts of selected impurity, such as arsenic, and used in solid-state electronic devices, eg. integrated circuits.

CHINESE INVENTIONS

Early discoveries of many useful things were made long ago in China, though some are described in modern books as Western inventions. This is because information has trickled only very slowly from China to the West. A good example is the magnetic compass. Lodestone compasses were first used in China in the 4th century BC. With this and many other devices, the Western world lacks information about the discoverers and we don't know just when breakthoughs were made. Here are some approximate dates as far as we know them.

BC

Plastic (lacquer) – 13th century

Plough – 6th century

Kite – 4th century

Poison gas – 4th century

Zero (the concept) – 4th century

Circadian rhythms in the human body – 2nd century

Circulation of the blood – 2nd century

Hot air balloon – 2nd century

Paper – 2nd century

Wheelbarrow – 1st century

Paper money – between 140 BC and 87 BC

AD

Rudder – 1st century

Suspension bridge – 1st century

Mast – 2nd century

Seismograph – 2nd century

Algebra - 3rd century

Cast iron - 4th century

Umbrella – towards the end of the 4th century

Matches – 6th century

Chess - 6th century

Brandy - 7th century

Whisky – 7th century

Printing – 8th century

Mechanical clock – 8th century

Musical timbre – 8th century

Gunpowder – 9th century

Playing cards – 9th century

Fireworks – 10th century

Flame thrower – 10th century

Spinning wheel – 11th century

Movable type – 11th century

The rocket – 12th century

The Chinese also invented the concept of negative numbers, and used decimals about 2300 years before the Western world adopted them. Despite this, the traditional method of computation by abacus may still be found practised in Chinese banks.

The Genius of China, 3000 years of science, discovery and invention, by Robert Temple, states that perhaps over half of the the basic discoveries and inventions employed in the modern world originated in China. Even Chinese people are generally unaware of this; when Jesuit missionaries showed some Chinese people a mechanical clock, they were awestruck, yet these clocks were invented in China.

In Britain it is widely believed that the circulation of the blood was discovered by William Harvey in 1628. In fact Harvey was not the first European to appreciate it. Other Europeans had read the writings of an Arab, al-Nefts of Damascus, who died in 1288. Al-Nefts in turn had got the idea from China.

BIBLIOGRAPHY

Asimov, Isaac, Asimov on Chemistry, London, MacDonald and James, 1975

Asimov, Isaac, Asimov's Guide to Science, Vol. 1, The Physical Sciences and Vol. 2, The Biological Sciences, London, Pelican, 1975

Atkins, P.W, The Creation, Oxford, W.H. Freeman, 1981

Ballard, Robert D. with Archbold, Rick, *The Discovery of the Titanic*, Toronto, Madison Press, 1987

Blackburn, David and Holster, Geoffrey (eds), *Hutchinson Encyclopaedia of Modern Technology*, London, Hutchinson, 1987

Briggs, Asa (consultant ed.), A Dictionary of Twentieth Century World Biography, Oxford, Oxford University Press, 1992

Bronowski, J, *The Ascent of Man*, London, BBC, 1973

Burns, Yvonne and Gunn, Pat, (eds.), *Down Syndrome: Moving Through Life*, London, Chapman and Hall, 1993

Carson, Neil R, Foundations of Physiological Psychology, Massachusetts, Allyn and Bacon, 1988

Cochrane, Jennifer, An Illustrated History of Medicine, London, Tiger Books International, 1996

Coleman, Andrew M., *What is Psychology? The Inside Story*, London, Hutchinson Educational, 1988

Coleman, V., The Medicine Men: Drugmakers, Doctors and Patients, London, Temple Smith, 1975

Cottrell, Philip D. (ed.), *Events - A Chronicle of the Twentieth Century*, London, Grange Books, 1994

Davidson, Frena Gray, *Alzheimer's*, London, Piatkus, 1995

Delpar, Helen (ed.), The Explorers: an Encyclopaedia of Explorers and Exploration, New York, McGraw Hill, 1980

Dixon B., Beyond the Magic Bullet, London, George Allen and Unwin, 1978

Douglas-Cooper, Helen (ed.), *Journeys of The Great Explorers*, Basingstoke, Automobile Association, 1992

The Encyclopaedia of Science in Action, (foreword by John Durant, London, MacMillan Reference Books, 1995

Evans, D.M.D. and Jones, J.B., Introduction to Medical Chemistry, London, Harper and Row, 1976

Eysenck, Hans, *Decline and Fall of the Freudian Empire*, Harmondsworth, Viking (an imprint of Penguin), 1985

Ferguson, Kitty, *Prisons of Light - Black Holes*, Cambridge, Cambridge University Press, 1996

Finniston, Monty (ed.), *Oxford Illustrated Encyclopaedia of Invention and Technology*, Oxford, Oxford University Press, 1992

Forsythe, Elizabeth, *The Mystery of Alzheimer's*, London, Kyle Cathie, 1996

Gavet-Imbert, Michèle (ed.), *The Guinness Book of Explorers and Exploration*, Enfield, Guinness Publishing, 1991

Gay, Peter (ed.), The Freud Reader, London, Vintage, 1995

Goodenough, Simon, *1500 Fascinating Facts About the Universe, the World and its People*, London, Treasure Press, 1983

Gould, Stephen jay, *Time's Arrow, Time's Cycle*, Harmondsworth, Penguin, 1991

Gracie, Archibald, *Titanic*, Gloucester, Alan Sutton Publishing, 1985

Green, John and Miller, David, AIDS – The Story of a Disease, London, Grafton Books, 1986

Gregory, Richard (ed.), *The Oxford Companion to the Mind*, Oxford, Oxford University Press, 1987

Harpur, Brian, *The Official Halley's Comet Book*, London, Hodder and Stoughton, 1985

Harré, Rom, *Great Scientific Experiments*, Oxford, Phaidon, 1981

Hawkes, Nigel, *AIDS*, London, Franklin Watts, 1987

Hawking, Stephen W., *A Brief History of Time*, London, Guild Publishing, 1990

Hawking, Stephen W., *Black Holes and Baby Universes*, London, Bantam Books, 1993

Hawking, Stephen W. and Penrose, Roger, *The Nature of Space and Time*, Princeton, Princeton University Press, 1996

Hazen, Robert M. and Trefil, James, Science Matters, London, Cassell, 1993

Kricher, John C., A Neotropical Companion, Princeton, Princeton University Press, 1987

K hne, Paul (trans. Jean Cunningham), *Medicine for the Layman*, London, Faber and Faber, 1957

Lancaster, Brian, *Mind, Brain and Human Potential*, Massachusetts, Element Inc., 1991

Magnusson, Magnus (consultant ed.), Reader's Digest Book of Facts, London, Reader's Digest Association, 1993

Margotta, Roberta, *The Hamlyn History of Medicine*, London, Hamlyn, 1996

Matthews, William H., *Geology Made Simple*, London, W.H. Allen, 1980

Miller, Carl, *The AIDS Handbook*, Harmondsworth, Penguin, 1990

Moore, Patrick, *The Unfolding Universe*, London, Michael Joseph, 1982

Morton, Ian and Ball, Judith, *Medicines, the Comprehensive Guide*, London, Bloomsbury Publishing, 1995

New Encyclopaedia Britannica, Vols I-XXIX, Chicago, Encyclopaedia Britannica Inc, 1994

Ousby, William J., *The Theory and Practice of Hypnotism*, London, Thorsons, 1990

Peacock, Roy E., *A Brief History of Eternity*, Eastbourne, Monarch Publications, 1989

Porter, Roy (ed.), *The Cambridge Illustrated History of Medicine*, Cambridge, Cambridge University Press, 1996

Pyke, Magnus and Moors, Patrick, *Everyman's Scientific Facts and Feats*, London, J.M. Dent, 1981

Roberts, Royston M., Serendipity: *Accidental Discoveries in Science*, New York, J.M. Wiley and Sons, 1989

Ronan, Colin, *The Universe Explained*, London, Thames and Hudson, 1994

Scammel, G.V., *The World Encompassed*, London, Methuen, 1937

Schwartz, Joseph and McGuinness, Michael, *Einstein for Beginners*, Cambridge, Icon Books, 1992

Spellerberg, Ian F. and Hardes, Steven R., *Biological Conservation*, Cambridge, Cambridge University Press, 1992

Stannard, Russell, *Science and Wonders*, London, Faber and Faber, 1996

Stine, William R., *Chemistry for the Consumer*, Boston, Allyn and Bacon Inc., 1978

Stratford, Brian, *Down's Syndrome, Past, Present and Future*, Harmondsworth, Penguin, 1989

Tattersfield, Donald, *Halley's Comet*, Oxford, Basil Blackwell, 1984

Tavanyar, Judy, *The Terence Higgins Trust HIV/AIDS Book*, London, Thorsons, 1992

Taylor, John, *When the Clock Struck Zero*, London, Picador, 1993

Temple, Robert, *The Genius of China, 3000 years of science, discovery and invention*, Andre Deutsch, 1991

Tibballs, Geoffrey, *The Guinness Book of Innovations*, Enfield, Guinness Publishing, 1994

Turner, Anthony C., *The Traveller's Health Guide*, Brentford, R. Lascelles, 1985

Waldrop, Mitchell M., *Complexity - the Emerging Science at the Edge of Order and Chaos*, Harmondsworth, Penguin, 1994

Walker, Eric and Williams, Glyn, 'Well Away: A Health Guide for Travellers' in the British Medical Journal, London, British Medical Association, 1988

Whitten, D.G.A. with Brooks, T.R.V., *The Penguin Dictionary of Geology*, Harmondsworth, Penguin, 1972

Who Was Who in The Twentieth Century, London, Dolphin Publications (an imprint of Bison Books), 1993

Wilcox, Desmond, *Explorers*, London, BBC, 1975

Williams, Trevor I., *A Short History of Twentieth Century Technology*, Oxford, Clarendon Press, 1982

Wilson, Derek, *The World Atlas of Treasure*, London, Collins, 1981

Wilson, D., *Penicillin in Perspective*, London, Faber and Faber, 1976

Wilson, Ian, *Undiscovered: the Fascinating World of Undiscovered Places, Graves, Wrecks and Treasures*, London, Chancellor Press, 1987

Wingate, Peter, *The Penguin Medical Encyclopaedia*, Harmondsworth, Penguin, 1982

Zakowich, Paul, *Culture Shock! A Traveller's Medical Guide*, London, Kuperard, 1996

Zim, Herbert and Shaffer, Paul, *Rocks and Minerals*, London, Paul Hamlyn, 1965

INDEX

Boolean Algebra
Boyle, Robert
Boyle's Law
Braconnot, Henri
Brazil from Portugal
Brown, Robert
Brownian Motion
Burnell, Jocelyn Bell
Burton, Richard

C

Cabral, Pedro Alvarez
Cape of Good Hope from Portugal
Capillaries
Carbon Dioxide
Carbon-60 (Buckminsterfullerene)
Carter, Howard
Cathode Rays
Cavendish, Henry
Caventou, Joseph Bienaimé
Cell Division
Cell Theory
Central and East Africa from
South Africa
Cerletti, Ugo
Chadwick, Sir James
Champollion, Jean François
Chaos Theory
Charles, Jacques
Charles' Law
Chemical Compositions of Stars
China from Italy
Chloroform as an Anaesthetic
Chlorophyll
Circulation of the Blood
Circumnavigation of the Earth
Clausius, Rudolf

Coelacanth
Coencas, Simon
Columbus, Christopher
Conditioned Reflexes
Conservation of Energy
Continental Drift
Cook, James
Cortés, Hernán Ferdinand
Cosmic Rays
Crick, Francis
Cullinan Diamond
Curie, Marie
Curie, Pierre

D

Da Gama, Vasco
Dalton, John
Dark matter
Dart, Raymond
Darwin, Charles
Davy, Sir Humphry
De Alcubierre, Rocco
De Dolomieu, Déodat
Dead Sea Scrolls
Decoding Hieroglyphics
Desideri, Ippolito
Deuterium
Di Varthema, Ludovico
Dias, Bartolemeu
Dirac, Paul
Dispersion of White Light
Distance of Moon from Earth
DNA and RNA
Doisy, Edward
Dolomitic Rock
Doppler Effect
Doppler, Christian

Down, John Langdon
Down's Syndrome
Drake, Sir Francis
Dubois, Eugene
Dutton, Clarence

E

Earth is a Magnet
Earth is Spherical
Earth's Circumference and Diameter
Easter Island from the Netherlands
Echo-sounding by Bats
Edh-Dhib, Mohammed
Edison Effect
Edison, Thomas
Ehrlich, Paul
Einstein, Albert
Electric Cell
Electric Current
Electroconvulsive Therapy (ECT)
Electromagnetic Induction
Electromagnetic Waves
Electromagnetism
Electron
Elements
Entropy
Eratosthenes
Erik the Red
Eriksson, Leif
Escapology
Evans, Sir Arthur
Expanding Universe

F

Fabry, Charles
Faraday, Michael

Feigenbaum, Mitchell
Fleming, Sir Alexander
Flemming, Walther
Food As A Source Of Energy
Fractional Dimensionality
Fraunhofer Lines
Freud, Sigmund
Frisch, Otto
Funk, Casimir

G

Gaia Theory
Galileo
Gallo, Robert
Galvani, Luigi
Gaulois Theory
Gaulois, Evariste
Gell-Mann, Murray
Germ Theory of Disease
Gilbert, William
Glacial Flow
Goldstein, Eugen
Gottlieb, Michael
Gravitation
Greenhouse Effect
Greenland from Iceland

H

Hahn, Otto
Hall, Marshall
Halley, Sir Edmond
Halley's Comet
Harrison, George
Hartog, Dirck
Hartwig, Ernst
Harvey, William

Heat is a Vibration
Heisenberg, Werner
Helium
Henle, Friedrich
Henry Dale, Sir
Heraclides of Pontius
Herophilus of Chalcedon
Hess, Victor
Hilbert Spaces
Hilbert, David
Hipparchus
HIV (Human Immunodeficiency Virus)
Hoffman, Albert
Homeostasis
Homo Erectus
Houdini, Harry
Hsüan-Tsang
Hubble, Edwin
Hughes, John
Hutton, James
Huygens, Christiaan
Hydrogen
Hypnosis

I

Ibn Battutah, Sheik Muhammad
Icarus
Imprinting
India from China
India from Portugal
Insects as Vectors of Disease
Insulin
Interference
Ions are Charged Atoms
Isotopes

J

Joliot-Curie, Irène and Frédéric
Jordanus Nemorarius
Jumping Genes
Jupiter's Satellites

K

Keesom, Anna
Keesom, Willem
Kekulé von Stradonitz, Friedrich
Kepler, Johannes
Knoop, Franz
Koch, Robert
Kosterlitz, Hans
Krebs Cycle
Krebs, Sir Hans
Kroto, Sir Harold

L

Laing, Alexander
Lake Tanganyika from England
Lake Victoria from England
Landsteiner, John
Langevin, Paul
Lascaux Cave Paintings
Laveran, Charles
Lavoisier, Antoine
Law of Falling Bodies
Laws of Electrolysis
Laws of Heredity
Laws of Motion
Laws of Planetary Motion
Le Verrier, Urbain
Leakey, Mary
Lemaître, Georges Henri

Lenard, Philipp
Leucippus of Miletus
Levene, Phoebus
Lhasa from Goa
Light has a Finite Speed
Lind, James
Lipmann, Fritz Albert
Livingstone, David
Lockyer, Sir Norman
Logan, William
Lorenz, Konrad
Lovelock, James
LSD as a Hallucinogen
Lyell, Sir Charles

M

Magellan, Ferdinand
Magnetism
Malpighi, Marcello
Mandelbrot, Benoit
Marco Polo
Marsal, Jacques
Maury, Matthew Fontaine
Maxwell, James Clerk
McClintock, Barbara
Mecca from Italy
Mechnikoff, Ilya
Meitner, Lise
Mendel, Gregor
Mendeleyev, Dmitri Ivanovich
Mesmer, Franz
Michel, Jean-Louis
Michell, John
Micro-Organisms
Minkowski, Hermann
Minoan Civilisation
Montagnier, Luc

Morgan, Thomas Hunt
Mouhot, Henri
Mount Kilimanjaro from Germany
Mountains of the Moon from the USA
Mycenae

N

Natural Opiates
Natural Selection
Neptune
Neutron
Newton, Sir Isaac
Niger River from Morocco
Nitrocellulose
Nuclear Fission
Nuclear Magnetic Resonance
(Magnetic Resonance Imaging)
Nucleotides in DNA

O

Oceanography
Oersted, Hans Christian
Ohm, George Simon
Ohm's Law
Olds, James
Onnes, Heike
Oort, Jan Hendrix
Origin of Coal
Oxygen
Ozone Layer

P

Pacific Islands from England
Pavlov, Ivan
Payne-Gaposchkin, Cecilia
Pelletier, Pierre Joseph

Penicillin

Periodic Table of Elements

Perkin, Sir William

Peru from Spain

Pfann, William

Phagocytosis

Photoelectric Effect

Piezoelectricity and Curie Temperature

Pizarro, Francisco

Planck, Max

Plasmodium Causes Malaria

Pleasure Centre

Plutonic Theory of Earth's Origin

Pompeii and Herculaneum

Positron

Precession of the Equinoxes

Priestley, Joseph

Proton

Psychoanalysis

Pulsars

Purcell, Edward Mills

Pythagoras

Q

Quantum Theory

Quarks

Quasars

R

Radioactivity

Radium and Polonium

Ravidat, Marcel

Rebmann, Johannes

Reflex Actions

Reflex Arcs

Relativity Theories

Respiration

Richet, Charles Robert

Riemann, Bernhard

Riemannian Geometry

Rockets

Roggeveen, Jacob

Rømer, Ole

Ross, Sir Ronald

Rotation of the Earth

Rutherford, Sir Ernest (Baron Rutherford)

S

Sahara Desert from Italy

Salvarsan

Sanger, Frederick

Scheele, Carl

Schleiden, Matthias

Schliemann, Heinrich

Schmidt, Maarten

Schönbein, Christian

Schwann, Theodor

Scurvy - Prevention and Cure

Seebeck, Thomas

Sequence of Amino Acids in Proteins

Sex Chromosomes

Sex Hormones

Shandera, Wayne

Sherrington, Sir Charles

Significance of Oxygen

Simpson, Sir James Young

Smith, J L B

Soddy, Frederick

South American Interior

Space-Time Continuum

Spallanzani, Lazaro

Speke, John

ND - #0494 - 270225 - C0 - 203/127/17 - PB - 9781861513014 - Matt Lamination